TECH
Timeout

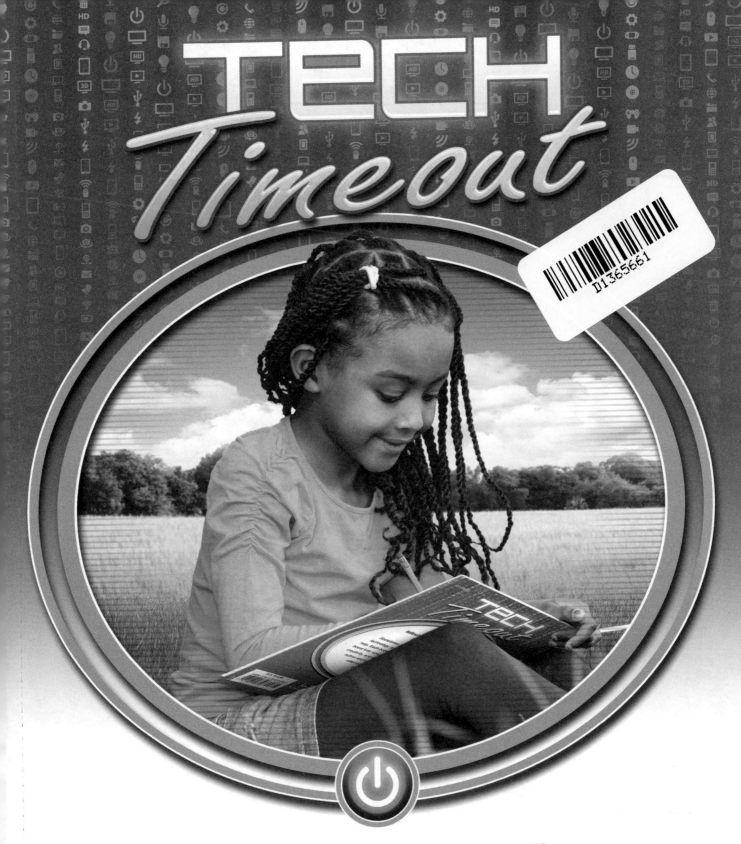

Second Grade

Thinking Kids™
Carson-Dellosa Publishing LLC
Greensboro, North Carolina

Thinking Kids™
Carson-Dellosa Publishing LLC
P.O. Box 35665
Greensboro, NC 27425 USA

ISBN 978-1-4838-2679-0

Table of Contents

Table of Contents

TECH *Timeout*

Grade 2

Are you ready for a tech timeout? The sections in this book have lots of ideas for activities that don't involve computers, smartphones, or TVs. Each activity provides plenty of screen-free fun.

As you go through this book, keep an eye out for red letters and this bird 🦅 scattered through the pages. You can keep track of them to complete activities at the end of the "Solve It" and "Find It" sections!

Create It

Get creative! You'll have a chance to glue, tape, draw, paint, snip, tear, and stack to complete a craft project. You may want to ask your parents to stock up on some of the following items that will be needed for this section: paper (including heavy paper, such as cardstock), colored construction paper, a roll of butcher paper or brown craft paper, crayons or markers, glue, tape (including masking tape or blue painter's tape), scissors, craft sticks, paint, brushes, cotton balls, stones, bubble wrap, yarn, and decorative stickers.

Solve It

The activities in this section require little more than a pencil and your brain. Many of the puzzles put your knowledge of words, numbers, and critical thinking to the test. Other puzzles require a keen sense of observation.

Find It

The hunt is on! Whether indoors, outdoors, or on the page, these activities will have you focused on tasks that require looking, finding, and collecting.

Play It

Time to get up and get moving! This section is filled with exercises and other physical activities to get your heart rate up and burn off energy. Whether it's running, hopping, dancing, or stretching, you are sure to get a healthy workout.

Create It

Tape Resist Painting

Peeling off the tape once your painting is dry is the best part of this project!

- **What You Need**
  - ❏ blue painter's tape or masking tape
  - ❏ heavy paper, such as cardstock or watercolor paper
  - ❏ paint
  - ❏ paintbrushes

- **What You Do**
  1. Make a design on your paper with strips of tape. You can do stripes, a crisscross pattern, or any other pattern you like.
  2. Paint the entire page. Be sure to cover any white areas. Paint right over the tape.
  3. Let your painting dry completely.
  4. When the paint is dry, carefully peel off the tape. The areas that were covered with tape will make a design.

If you like, try this project again—but this time, spell out your name in tape.

Make Your Own Constellation

A constellation is a group of stars that seem to form an image. In this project, you get to make and name your own constellation!

● **What You Need**

❏ black construction paper

❏ a white crayon or colored pencil

❏ gold star stickers (or a metallic gold pen)

● **What You Do**

1. Draw a large, simple picture on black paper with a white crayon or colored pencil. Some ideas are: a tree, a butterfly, a bird, a flower, a bone, an anchor, a hand, or an animal.

2. If you have gold stars, place them on the drawing so it looks like the drawing is connecting the stars. You can also draw the stars with a gold pen.

3. Name your constellation.

If you like, come up with an original story that goes with your constellation. Tell your story to your family. Ask them if they know the stories of any real constellations. If they don't, see if you can work together to find some stories online.

Cardboard Tube Owls

Cardboard tubes are great for doing all sorts of crafts. Feel free to experiment with making other creatures as well.

● **What You Need**

- ❑ empty toilet paper tubes
- ❑ paint
- ❑ paintbrushes
- ❑ patterned paper or fabric
- ❑ glue
- ❑ scissors
- ❑ googly eyes or black marker

● **What You Do**

1. Paint the cardboard tubes any color (or colors) you'd like.

2. Give the paint some time to dry. While it dries, cut out a triangle beak and wings for your owl from the paper or fabric.

3. Push down on one side of the top of the painted tube. Then, push down on the other side. The edges of the tube will point up to make your owl's ears.

4. Glue the beak and wings onto your owl.

5. If you are using googly eyes, glue them on. If not, you can draw eyes with a black marker.

Puffy Ice Cream Cone

This ice-cream treat looks good enough to eat, but it's made of shaving cream, so don't try it!

● **What You Need**

- ❏ glue
- ❏ shaving cream
- ❏ food coloring
- ❏ a plastic cup
- ❏ a paintbrush
- ❏ scissors
- ❏ a piece of heavy paper, such as cardstock or construction paper
- ❏ a brown paper bag
- ❏ a marker

● **What You Do**

1. Cut out a cone shape from the brown paper bag.

2. Draw crisscross lines on the cone with a marker. Your cone will look like this:

3. Glue the cone to your paper

4. In the plastic cup, squirt a mound of shaving cream. Add about a tablespoon of glue.

5. Mix the glue and shaving cream together. Add a couple of drops of food coloring (red for strawberry ice cream, green for mint, red and blue for grape, and so on).

6. Use the paintbrush to draw a scoop (or two or three) of ice cream on your cone.

You can also make an ice cream sundae with the puffy paint. What will you use for toppings?

Flower Pot Can

Fill this pretty pot with some soil and a real plant, and give it as a gift!

● **What You Need**

- ❑ an empty can
- ❑ glue
- ❑ a plastic cup
- ❑ a paintbrush
- ❑ tissue paper (patterned, if you have it)
- ❑ ribbon (optional)

● **What You Do**

1. Make sure your can is clean and dry.

2. Pour some glue into the plastic cup. Add a small amount of water to thin it.

3. Cut a piece of tissue paper that will fit around the can. It should be a little longer than the can so you can fold it over the top and bottom.

4. Paint the outside of the can with a thin layer of glue.

5. Carefully wrap the tissue around the can. Smooth it on. Be sure to glue and fold over the pieces at the top and bottom of the can.

6. If your tissue paper does not have a pattern, you can add one yourself. Cut or tear a few scraps of tissue in another color. Glue them onto the first layer in an interesting design.

7. Brush a thin coat of glue over the outside of the tissue paper.

8. Let the can dry. If you like, tie a ribbon around it.

Add some soil and a small plant. You have a cheerful decoration for your home, or a nice gift for a friend!

Leaf Designs

Collect your favorite kinds of leaves to make this colorful nature picture. Use all sorts of shapes, sizes, and colors of leaves.

● **What You Need**

- ❏ fresh leaves in various shapes and sizes
- ❏ watercolor paints in fall leaf colors
- ❏ paintbrushes
- ❏ pencil
- ❏ black crayon
- ❏ white construction paper

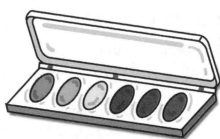

● **What You Do**

1. With your pencil, trace the outlines of leaves onto white construction paper. Make sure to fill the entire page.

2. Trace over each leaf shape with a thick line of black crayon.

3. Paint the inside of each leaf shape with different fall colors. The black crayon will keep the colors from running together.

Tree Cork Painting

If you don't have any corks at home, you can easily find them at most craft stores.

● **What You Need**

- ❑ 1–4 corks
- ❑ paint in fall colors (red, yellow, orange, brown)
- ❑ a paper plate
- ❑ heavy paper, such as cardstock or construction paper (in white or light blue)
- ❑ a brown marker or crayon (optional)

● **What You Do**

1. Draw or paint a tree trunk and branches on your paper.
2. Squeeze some of each of your paints onto the paper plate.
3. If you have only one cork, you'll need to rinse or wipe it off between colors.
4. Use the cork to stamp "leaves" on the branches of your tree. Space the different colors out around the tree.
5. If you like, paint or draw some other details on your painting (like clouds, grass, animals, and so on).

Can you do make the tree again but in a different season? You could use the corks to make light green leaves and pale pink blossoms for spring. Or, you could make green leaves and red apples. What other details could you paint with the cork stamps?

Rainy Day Clouds

This is a good craft for spring, when there are lots of rainy days.

- ● **What You Need**
  - ❏ heavy white paper, like cardstock
  - ❏ a pencil
  - ❏ cotton balls
  - ❏ glue
  - ❏ light blue paper
  - ❏ tape
  - ❏ yarn (in blue or white, if possible) or string

- ● **What You Do**
  1. Draw two large clouds on the white paper. Your clouds should be shaped something like this: .
  2. Cut out the clouds.
  3. Spread glue lightly on the clouds, and cover them with cotton balls.
  4. Cut out raindrops from the blue paper. Your raindrops should be shaped something like this: . You will need about eight or 10 drops for each cloud.
  5. Poke two small holes in the bottom of each cloud. The holes should be spaced several inches apart.
  6. Thread a piece of string or yarn through each hole and knot it in the back.
  7. Glue several raindrops onto each string. Let the glue dry completely.

It's time to display your rainy day clouds! They will look especially nice hung near a window—on a cloudy or a sunny day!

Box Guitar

You can make a guitar with things you have around the house. You'll be strumming tunes in no time!

● **What You Need**

- ❏ a shoebox (no lid needed)
- ❏ rubber bands of varying widths
- ❏ tempera paint
- ❏ paintbrushes with stiff bristles
- ❏ paper towel roll
- ❏ glue

● **What You Do**

1. Paint the paper towel roll and entire shoebox, a few sides at a time, with a dark brown color. Let it dry.

2. Paint over the dark brown with lighter brown paint. This makes it look like wood. Let it dry.

3. Glue the paper towel roll to a short end of the shoebox.

4. Stretch rubber bands around the open shoebox. Space them out evenly, from the widest to the narrowest band.

5. Experiment by plucking the strings one at a time, as well as by strumming the strings all at once.

Starry Night Scene

Draw the stars and planets in the night sky. This project sparkles even more with fluorescent or glitter crayons.

- **What You Need**
  - ❑ watercolor paint
  - ❑ paintbrush (a flat 1-inch brush works best)
  - ❑ crayons
  - ❑ white construction paper
  - ❑ poster board or heavy paper
  - ❑ scissors

- **What You Do**

  1. Draw and cut out several star shapes from the poster board to use as stencils or patterns to trace.

  2. Use crayons to trace your stars and draw a night sky design on the paper. Make sure to draw enough stars to fill the entire page. Color heavily.

  3. Use dark blue or black watercolors to paint over the entire paper. Paint over your design only one time.

  4. Add planets, moons, shooting stars, or anything else you can think of to your starry night.

Yarn Doll

Did you know you could make your own doll? All you need are a few materials you probably have on hand.

- **What You Need**
  - ❑ yarn
  - ❑ scissors
  - ❑ a piece of cardboard (about 8 inches by 8 inches)

- **What You Do**
  1. Wind the yarn lengthwise around the cardboard one time.
  2. Tie a knot at the top.
  3. Continue wrapping the yarn around the cardboard. You'll need to do this about 100 times.
  4. Tie the end of the yarn to one of the loops.
  5. Cut a small piece of yarn. Tie it at the top of your loop, near the top of the cardboard.
  6. Slide the yarn off the cardboard.
  7. Cut another small piece of yarn. Tie it about 1 inch from the top of the yarn. This will be the doll's neck.
  8. Make the doll's arms by pulling out a few loops of yarn on either side.
  9. Leave the arms out, and tie a small piece of yarn around the middle of the main piece. This will be the doll's waist.
  10. Make small ties at each of the wrists. Trim the loops of yarn for the hands.
  11. Cut the large loop at the very bottom to make the skirt. For a boy doll, divide the skirt into two pieces to make legs. Make small ties at the ankles.

If you like, you can braid the arms and legs for a boy doll. Leave the legs unbraided for a girl doll.

Build-a-Face Stones

These fun stones are simple to make, and the combinations of faces you can create are endless!

● **What You Need**

❏ stones with a flat surface in different sizes

❏ paints

❏ paintbrushes

● **What You Do**

1. Sort out the stones you have. Create piles of stones that will make good eyes, noses, and mouths.

2. Use the paints to make eyes, noses, and mouths on your stones. Try to make different expressions and emotions (scared, happy, surprised, sad, and so on).

3. Once the paint is dry, arrange your rocks to make faces.

4. If a friend or family member can work with you, take turns making up stories about the different characters you create.

If you like this activity, you can do some different versions. Make animal faces, alien or monster faces, or add fun features to your human faces (like mustaches, goatees, bows, and so on).

Bubble Wrap Printing

This activity makes lovely, unique wrapping paper.

● **What You Need**

❏ bubble wrap

❏ tape

❏ a can (the size of a soup can)

❏ a paper plate

❏ a roll of butcher paper or brown craft paper

❏ paint

❏ paintbrushes

● **What You Do**

1. Cover the top of a can with a piece of bubble wrap.

2. Tape down the sides of the bubble wrap.

3. Unroll the butcher paper or craft paper. Tape the edge of it to your work surface so it doesn't roll up.

4. Squeeze some paint onto the paper plate.

5. Dip the bubble wrap into the paint. You may want to make your first print on a piece of scrap paper.

6. Press the bubble wrap onto the paper to make prints. Dip it again when you need to.

7. If you like, switch colors after a while.

8. Let the paper dry completely before you use it (or roll it back up to save as gift wrap).

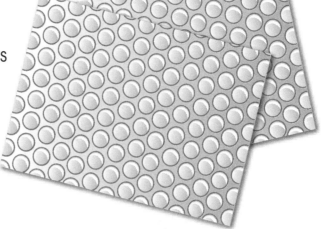

Nature Photo Collage

As you gather the natural materials for this project, think about how you will be able to use them.

● **What You Need**

- ❏ several photos of yourself (larger photos work better)
- ❏ glue or a glue stick
- ❏ cardstock or construction paper
- ❏ scissors
- ❏ natural items, like leaves, flowers, petals, small twigs, acorn caps, and so on

● **What You Do**

1. Cut out pictures of yourself (or family and friends) from the photos. Check with an adult first to make sure this is okay.

2. Glue the images to your paper.

3. Now, it's time to decorate! Use the natural items to make skirts, hats, antenna, silly hairdos, or shoes for yourself. Glue them in place. You can even make a landscape or background—like clouds made from dandelion puffs, or a hillside made from grass clippings.

Clothespin Caterpillars

These cute caterpillars take only a few minutes to make. And they'll never turn into butterflies!

● **What You Need**

❑ wooden clothespins

❑ pompoms

❑ pipe cleaners

❑ googly eyes

❑ glue

❑ scissors

● **What You Do**

1. Glue pompoms along the top of the clothespin. Try to cover the wood completely.

2. Cut off small pieces of pipe cleaners to make antennas.

3. Add a dab of glue to each antenna, and poke it into the first pompom.

4. Glue on googly eyes.

5. Let the glue on your caterpillars dry before you use them.

Use these cute clothespins to display artwork in your room. You could also make a garland of your artwork and display it using the clothespins.

Origami Sailboat

Origami is the ancient art of folding paper. Amazing creations can be made without even cutting or gluing.

- ● **What You Need**
    - ❏ construction paper or any unlined paper
    - ❏ crayons or markers
    - ❏ scissors
    - ❏ a ruler

- ● **What You Do**
    1. Cut the construction paper into a square with 4-inch sides.
    2. Fold your paper in half diagonally, and then fold it in half diagonally again.
    3. Unfold the paper once to make a triangle.
    4. Fold one edge up to meet the halfway line (see diagram on the right).
    5. Fold the bottom corners on the boat back behind, as shown. Tuck them in together to keep them in place.
    6. Decorate your sail with crayons or markers.
    7. Give your boat a name! Write it on the side.

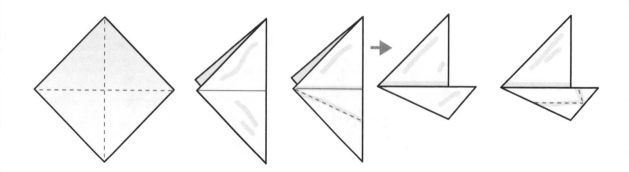

Rocky Turtle

Make a beautiful mosaic with pebbles for your turtle's shell.

● **What You Need**

- ❏ a paper plate
- ❏ brown paint
- ❏ a paintbrush
- ❏ scissors
- ❏ green construction paper
- ❏ small rocks or pebbles
- ❏ glue

● **What You Do**

1. Before you begin, go outside and search for some small pebbles. If you have some among your craft supplies, you can use them instead.

2. Paint the back side of the paper plate brown.

3. While the paint dries, cut out a head and four legs for your turtle.

4. Glue the head and legs onto the paper plate from underneath, so they stick out.

5. Glue the pebbles onto the back of the turtle to make its shell.

Drip Painting

You will need a little patience for this project, but you'll love the results!

● **What You Need**

- ❏ heavy paper, such as cardstock or watercolor paper (or a canvas)
- ❏ a piece of cardboard slightly bigger than your paper
- ❏ masking tape
- ❏ paints
- ❏ newspaper

● **What You Do**

1. Spread out newspaper to cover your work area. This project can be messy!

2. Place the paper on top of the cardboard. Hold it in place with a couple of small pieces of masking tape.

3. Squeeze paint in several places near the top of your paper.

4. Tip the paper so that the paint drips down. Be patient and let it drip as far as it can.

5. Add some more paint to empty spaces on your paper. Let the paint drip again. If you like, tip the paper in a different direction this time.

6. When most or all of your paper is covered, set it someplace safe to dry.

7. When your painting is dry, remove the tape and display your artwork!

Monster Sock Puppet

Turn your sock into a monster! Make your monster any animal or creature imaginable. Be creative! Give your monster a name.

- ● **What You Need**
  - ❑ sock
  - ❑ red felt or fabric oval
  - ❑ fabric scraps (any colors)
  - ❑ fabric scissors
  - ❑ craft glue (try to use glue made especially for fabric)

- ● **What You Do**
  1. Put one hand in the sock to find where the mouth should be. Your thumb should make the bottom jaw of the monster's mouth.
  2. Glue the red fabric oval where the mouth is formed.
  3. Cut out eyes, ears, and anything else you want on your monster from the fabric scraps.
  4. Glue them on the puppet any way you like.

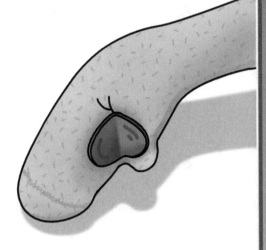

Yarn Art

Weaving is a cinch with just a few materials in this fun craft.

- **What You Need**
  - ❏ a piece of cardboard
  - ❏ scissors
  - ❏ yarn (in one or more colors)
  - ❏ a pencil
  - ❏ a cup

- **What You Do**

  1. Place the cup upside down on the cardboard. Trace the circle with a pencil.

  2. If the cardboard is hard to cut, ask for an adult's help to cut out the circle.

  3. Now, cut small slits in the cardboard all the way around the circle. The slits should be about $\frac{1}{2}$-inch long. You can decide how many to do, but you should have at least a dozen. Try to space them evenly around the circle.

  4. Take a piece of yarn and thread it through one slit.

  5. Flip the circle over and pull the yarn across to a slit on the opposite side. Thread it through that slit.

  6. Pull the yarn across the circle underneath, to a slit on the opposite side.

  7. Continue this pattern until you are happy with the way your circle looks. Tuck the loose ends under the weaving.

  8. Find a place where you can hang your weaving to display it. If you like, thread a small piece of yarn through a loop on the top to make it easy to hang.

Craft Stick Harmonica

What tune will you play on your new harmonica?

● **What You Need**

- ❏ two large craft sticks
- ❏ two rubber bands
- ❏ a strip of paper
- ❏ two toothpicks
- ❏ scissors

● **What You Do**

1. Ask an adult to cut the toothpicks so that they are the width of the craft sticks.

2. Cut out a piece of paper about the same size as the craft sticks.

3. Place the paper on one of the sticks. Put the other stick on top.

4. Wrap one rubber band around one end of the two craft sticks.

5. Slip a toothpick in between the two craft sticks. Slide it down until it is next to the rubber band.

6. Repeat steps 4 and 5 at the other end of the craft sticks.

7. Now, it's time to make music! Hold the two ends of the crafts sticks and blow. You can also try to suck in air. Experiment with the different sounds you can make.

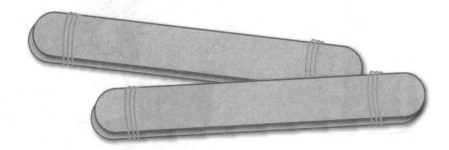

Sand Painting

Create a colorful beach in a jar! Sand paintings are fun to make and easy to clean up.

● **What You Need**

- ❏ sand (white sand from garden shops works best)
- ❏ baby food jar or another glass jar with a lid
- ❏ food coloring
- ❏ paper cups
- ❏ spoon
- ❏ a ruler

● **What You Do**

1. Fill paper cups about three-quarters full of sand.

2. Add a few drops of food coloring to each cup and mix well. Prepare at least three different colors of sand.

3. Carefully spoon the sand into the jar, forming one layer of color at a time.

4. When the jar is full, screw on the lid tightly.

After you fill your jar, take a toothpick and slowly poke into the sand along the sides. This will create wavy lines of different colors without completely mixing them.

Circle Art

When this painting is finished, it will look like a modern work of art!

- **What You Need**
  - ❏ a plastic cup
  - ❏ black paint
  - ❏ a paper plate
  - ❏ heavy paper, such as cardstock or watercolor paper
  - ❏ watercolors
  - ❏ a paintbrush
  - ❏ a cup of water

- **What You Do**
  1. Squirt some black paint onto a paper plate and spread it out.
  2. Dip the open end of the plastic cup into the paint.
  3. Press the cup to the paper to make a print.
  4. Continue making circle prints, overlapping your circles.
  5. Let the black circles dry for a few minutes.
  6. Fill in the circles (and parts of circles) with watercolor paints.

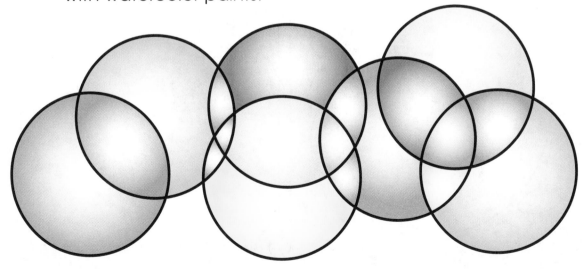

Fill in the Frames

Fill in the frames below with your own drawings. You can do portraits of people or animals, pictures of nature or a favorite toy, or even abstract pictures. Have fun, and let your imagination go!

Egg Carton Wreath

This beautiful wreath is easy to make and is a cheerful decoration for spring.

- **What You Need**
    - ❏ a cardboard egg carton
    - ❏ scissors
    - ❏ a paper plate
    - ❏ paints
    - ❏ paintbrushes
    - ❏ glue
    - ❏ yarn or ribbon (optional)

- **What You Do**
    1. Cut the inner circle out of the paper plate. Paint the plate green.
    2. Cut some leaf shapes out of the inner circle from the paper plate. Paint them green, too.
    3. Carefully cut out the cups from the egg carton. Then, cut along the top edge of each cup to add some petals.
    4. Paint each of the cups. You can paint them all the same color or several different colors.
    5. Paint a colored center for each flower.
    6. Glue the flowers and the leaves to the green wreath shape you made.

If you like, tie some yarn or a ribbon to the top of the wreath to make it easy to hang.

Collage Silhouette

If you have trouble thinking of a shape to use for this project, ask an adult to help you find one online.

- **What You Need**
  - ❏ two pieces of cardstock or construction paper
  - ❏ scissors
  - ❏ papers with different patterns and colors
  - ❏ a pencil
  - ❏ a glue stick

- **What You Do**
  1. Draw a large, simple shape on a piece of paper. Some ideas are a flower, a star, a fish, a moon, a butterfly, a house, or a leaf.
  2. Cut the shape out from the center of the paper.
  3. Use the cut-out page as a stencil to trace your shape onto the other sheet of paper.
  4. Cut out lots of thin strips of paper from your patterned papers.
  5. Glue the strips onto the paper on which you traced your stencil.
  6. Now, place the cut-out page on top of the paper with all the patterned strips on it.
  7. Use the glue stick to glue it in place.

You can make this collage as a beautiful card for a family member, or you can use it to decorate your room.

If you like, do this project again near a holiday. Just use a pine tree, a heart, a bunny, a shamrock, or a turkey for your silhouette!

Veggie Drawings

Use veggies to kickstart your imagination and come up with some fun drawings.

● **What You Need**

  ❑ several pieces of vegetables—whole or sliced (check with a parent first)

  ❑ paper

  ❑ pencils and/or colored pencils

● **What You Do**

  1. Place a vegetable (or a slice of one) on your paper. What does it remind you of? A smile, a balloon, a tree? Make a drawing around the veggie.

  2. If you make a series of these, see if you can connect them together with a story. Ask a friend or family member to listen to your veggie-illustrated story.

You can also experiment with fruits and other foods, such as pasta, beans, and cereal. Just be sure to get an okay from an adult first.

Nature Crown

Make a beautiful crown with treasures you find outside.

● **What You Need**

❑ a brown paper bag

❑ scissors

❑ duct tape or wide masking tape

❑ natural items, like leaves, flowers, grasses, feathers, and so on

❑ a measuring tape

❑ a pencil

● **What You Do**

1. Cut open the brown bag.

2. Measure your head with the measuring tape.

3. Cut out a strip of the brown paper bag that is about 1 inch longer than your head measurement. The strip should be about 4 inches tall.

4. Use the pencil to make zigzag lines along the top of the paper strip. It should look something like this: ⋁⋀⋁

5. Cut a piece of tape that is the same length as your paper strip.

6. Place it on top of the paper with the sticky side up.

7. Carefully overlap one end of the strip with the other to form a crown.

8. Stick your leaves, flowers, and feathers to your crown.

Make a Rainstick

Some ancient cultures believed that rainsticks could cause rain. What do you think? Here's how you can give it a try!

- **What You Need**
  - ❏ a long cardboard tube (like one from a roll of gift wrap)
  - ❏ duct tape
  - ❏ dried beans
  - ❏ markers and/or stickers
  - ❏ tinfoil (optional)

- **What You Do**
  1. Seal one end of the tube with tape. Make sure the tape is secure.
  2. Carefully pour some beans into the tube. Give it a gentle shake to see if you like the sound. If you don't, add some more beans.
  3. If you want to slow the beans down, make a long crumpled stick of tinfoil, and add it to the tube.
  4. Seal the other end of the tube with tape.
  5. Decorate your rainstick with designs, pictures, or stickers.
  6. Now, you're ready to make it rain! Tip the tube, and listen to the sound of the beans falling.

Experiment with the sounds of your rainstick. Does it make a different sound when you tip it over slowly? Quickly?

Lemon Juice Watercolors

Lemon juice has an interesting effect on watercolor paints. Try this activity to find out what it is!

● **What You Need**

- ❏ heavy paper, such as cardstock or watercolor paper
- ❏ watercolors or liquid watercolors
- ❏ a cup of water
- ❏ a paintbrush
- ❏ lemon juice
- ❏ paper towel
- ❏ an eyedropper (optional)
- ❏ a dark marker (optional)

● **What You Do**

1. Cover your paper with watercolors. Apply the color fairly thickly. It's fine to overlap the colors or let them bleed together. You can paint a picture or just make a design.

2. Use an eyedropper to drip lemon juice onto the painting. If your lemon juice comes in a squeeze bottle, you can just squeeze drops onto your painting.

3. Let the juice sit for a minute or two.

4. Now, dab at the juice with a piece of paper towel. The lemon juice will leave behind interesting bleached-out spots.

What do the lighter spots look like? If you like, you can turn them into things with your marker. Do you see a flower? A squirrel? A skyscraper? A tree? A truck? Add details to finish the picture.

Rainbow Scratchboard

Have you ever scratched a design on special paper that has a rainbow hiding underneath? It's time to make your own magical paper!

● **What You Need**

- ❏ a piece of cardboard (one side of a cereal box works well)
- ❏ scissors
- ❏ crayons in different colors
- ❏ a black crayon
- ❏ a paper clip

● **What You Do**

1. Cut out a piece of cardboard, such as one side of a cereal box.

2. Color the whole piece of cardboard with crayons. Be sure not to leave any parts uncolored. Use lots of different colors of crayons.

3. Now, color over the colored area with a black crayon. Color thickly so that you cannot see any of the colors below.

4. Use the paper clip to scratch a design onto the cardboard. Anywhere you scratch off the black crayon, the bright colors will be visible.

If you make a mistake, don't worry! Just color over the area with the black crayon. Then, scratch off a new design.

Snowy Painting

Your snowy scene looks almost real with this project. Create another background scene for a completely different picture!

● **What You Need**

- ❏ dark blue or black construction paper
- ❏ construction paper in other colors
- ❏ thick, white tempera paint
- ❏ small sponge
- ❏ cotton balls
- ❏ pie pan
- ❏ aluminum foil
- ❏ glue
- ❏ scissors

● **What You Do**

1. Cut colored construction paper into various sizes of triangles, squares, and rectangles.

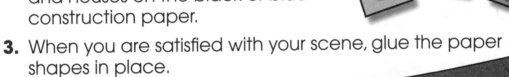

2. Use the shapes to create buildings and houses on the black or blue construction paper.

3. When you are satisfied with your scene, glue the paper shapes in place.

4. Cut out window shapes from aluminum foil and glue them to the buildings.

5. Pour a small amount of white tempera paint into a paper plate.

6. Dip a sponge in the paint, and then blot the paint gently onto the paper to create snow.

7. Stretch cotton balls across the bottom of the paper to make more snow. Glue them in place.

Butterfly Nature Collage

This pretty butterfly collage is the perfect way to welcome spring.

- **What You Need**

  - ❏ construction paper
  - ❏ scissors
  - ❏ glue or a glue stick
  - ❏ natural materials, like flower petals, stems, leaves, and grasses

- **What You Do**

  1. Draw a large, simple butterfly on a piece of construction paper. It should take up most of the page. Your butterfly should look something like this:

  2. Cut out the butterfly.

  3. Glue your natural materials onto the butterfly's wings to make a design. Try to make your design symmetrical (the same on both sides), the way a real butterfly would be.

Stems or long grasses make nice antennas. Flower petals and small leaves are great for making designs on the wings.

Create a Creature

It's time to get silly! What sort of wild or goofy creature will you come up with?

● **What You Need**
- ☐ old magazines or catalogs
- ☐ a glue stick
- ☐ plain paper or construction paper
- ☐ a pencil
- ☐ scissors

● **What You Do**

1. Flip through the magazines to look for pictures of animals. You can also look for vehicles or humans.

2. Cut out the pictures you find and look for ways to combine them. For example, you could combine a giraffe's head and neck with the body of a girl, and the wheels of a pickup truck.

3. Once you've come up with a combination you like, glue it to the paper.

4. Write a name for the creature you've created.

If you like, write a story to go along with your picture. Share it with a friend or family member.

Eggheads

Make your own egg pal with just a few simple materials!

● **What You Need**

- ❏ one or more uncooked eggs
- ❏ a bowl
- ❏ a dinner knife
- ❏ markers
- ❏ paper towel or cotton balls
- ❏ seeds (grass, wheat grass, or cress work well)
- ❏ glue (optional)
- ❏ googly eyes (optional)

● **What You Do**

1. Hold the egg over the bowl. Use the dinner knife to chip a hole out of the top. Chip way with the knife (or use your fingers), until you have removed about the top quarter of the shell.

2. Pour the raw egg into the bowl. Put it in the refrigerator. (Maybe you can have scrambled eggs for dinner!)

3. Carefully wash the eggshell with soap and water. Wash your hands well, too.

4. Once the shell is dry, draw a face on it.

5. If you like, you can glue on the googly eyes.

6. Tear up some paper towel, and set it inside the shell. If you like, you can use a couple of cotton balls instead.

7. Drip in a bit of water to make the towel or cotton balls damp.

8. Sprinkle in some seeds.

9. Set your eggshell in a sunny window. Be sure to keep it damp but not wet.

10. In a few days, your seeds will sprout. The seedlings will look like hair on your funny face!

Rolled Paper Collage

This project is a great way to recycle old magazines and catalogs.

● **What You Need**

- ❏ old catalogs or magazines
- ❏ a glue stick
- ❏ a piece of cardboard (cereal boxes work well)
- ❏ scissors

● **What You Do**

1. Cut a piece of cardboard about the size of a sheet of paper or slightly smaller.
2. Cut out a number of strips from magazines or catalogs. The width of the strips is not important.
3. Roll the strips, and seal the edges with a glue stick to make paper tubes.
4. Once you have a large pile of tubes, you can begin arranging them. Lay them out beside the cardboard.
5. Cover part of the cardboard with glue. Then, begin placing the tubes on the cardboard.
6. Allow the glue to dry before you display your artwork.

If you like, try to cut out strips that are mostly a single color (mostly red or mostly blue, for example). Then, you can arrange them by color in your collage.

String Art

Have you heard of abstract art? Instead of representing something real, it is made up of interesting colors, lines, and shapes. Try making your own abstract art with this painting project.

● **What You Need**

- ❏ string or yarn
- ❏ scissors
- ❏ paints
- ❏ a paper plate
- ❏ heavy paper, such as cardstock or watercolor paper

● **What You Do**

1. Cut several pieces of string or yarn.
2. Squeeze the paint colors you want to use onto a paper plate.
3. Dip a piece of the string into the paint.
4. Drag the string across your paper. Dip it back in the same color and repeat, or use a new piece of string.
5. Continue the process until you are happy with the way your artwork looks.

If you like, try this project again. This time, use paints in different shades of the same color (like all greens, or all blues).

Natural Paint Brushes

You can create some one-of-a-kind art by making your own paintbrushes.

- **What You Need**
  - ❑ several small sticks that are at least as wide around as one of your fingers
  - ❑ rubber bands
  - ❑ natural materials, such as pinecones, grasses, pine needles, moss, flowers, and so on
  - ❑ paints
  - ❑ heavy paper, such as cardstock or watercolor paper

- **What You Do**
  1. Find materials outside that you think might make interesting paintbrushes.
  2. Using a rubber band, attach each material to the top of a small stick.
  3. Dip your brushes in paint and experiment with making marks. Do some work better than others? Are some better for making finer marks?
  4. Create a painting using the brushes you made.

See if your family can guess what kinds of materials you used for each of your brushes.

Quick and Easy Puppets

These are some of the fastest puppets you can make!

● **Greeting Card Puppet**

❏ Cut out a person or animal from a greeting card.

❏ Glue it onto a craft stick or a plastic drinking straw for an instant puppet.

● **Cardboard Roll People Puppet**

❏ Draw a face on a cardboard roll.

❏ Add a paper baking cup skirt by cutting out the bottom of a cup and then gluing it to the roll.

❏ Glue on yarn or cotton balls for hair and baking cups or paper scraps for hats and other simple features.

● **Envelope Shark Puppet**

❏ Seal a long, business-sized envelope.

❏ Cut a triangle from one of the short edges to make a mouth.

❏ Tape the triangle to the top for the fin.

❏ Trim off the edge of the envelope opposite the mouth, making an opening for your hand.

❏ Decorate your shark with eyes, stripes, and sharp teeth!

● **Paper Plate Puppet**

❏ Glue or draw a face onto a paper plate. You may want to use yarn hair, button eyes, ribbon eyebrows, and so on.

❏ When everything is dry, tape a wooden paint stirring stick to the back of the plate.

Fishbowl

Would you like to have a pet that you don't have to feed or walk? Make one yourself with this fun craft.

● **What You Need**

❏ a paper plate

❏ blue paint

❏ a paintbrush

❏ small pebbles or dry white beans

❏ glue and a glue stick

❏ construction paper

❏ green tissue paper (optional)

❏ markers (optional)

● **What You Do**

1. Paint the paper plate blue.

2. While the paint is drying, cut out a fish or two from construction paper. If you like, you can decorate them with markers.

3. Make a water plant for your fishbowl. You can make it out of green construction paper or tissue paper.

4. Glue the beans or small pebbles to the bottom third of the paper plate.

5. Glue on the fish and water plant. Your fishbowl is complete! Display it in your room or someplace where your family can enjoy it.

Styrofoam Printing

You can make an endless number of prints with just one printing plate.

● **What You Need**

- ❏ a foam tray (such as a clean meat tray from the grocery store)
- ❏ a pencil (dull works better than sharp)
- ❏ construction paper
- ❏ paint
- ❏ a paper plate
- ❏ a foam paintbrush

● **What You Do**

1. Draw a picture or a pattern on the foam tray with the dull pencil.

2. Squirt paint onto the paper plate.

3. Paint your foam tray with the foam brush.

4. Turn it face down, and press it firmly onto the construction paper. Lift it up, and you'll see your print!

5. To make more prints, just rinse the foam tray and paint it another color.

Dream Catcher

Some Native American groups believe that a dream catcher can catch any bad dreams you might have. Here's how to make a dream catcher that you can hang above your own bed.

- ● **What You Need**
  - ❏ a paper plate
  - ❏ a single-hole punch
  - ❏ yarn
  - ❏ scissors
  - ❏ markers or colored pencils
  - ❏ tape
  - ❏ plastic beads and feathers (optional)

- ● **What You Do**
  1. Cut out the inner circle from the paper plate.
  2. Decorate the outer ring of the plate with the markers or colored pencils.
  3. Use the hole punch to punch holes around the inner ring of the plate. The holes should be about an inch apart.
  4. Take a piece of yarn and tape it to the back of the paper plate ring.
  5. Thread the other end through one of the holes. Then, stretch it across the plate and thread it through another hole. Continue weaving back and forth across the plate.
  6. When you are done weaving, tape the other end of the yarn to the back of the plate.
  7. If you like, punch a couple more holes at the bottom of the plate. Tie yarn through the holes. Then, string beads on the yarn. Finish beaded strings with a feather.

Put up your dream catcher in your room, and see if it works!

Crinkle Paper Art

You won't believe how simple it is to get this project started! But finishing it takes a bit more patience.

- **What You Need**
  - ❏ white paper
  - ❏ markers (including a black marker)

- **What You Do**
  1. Crumple up a piece of plain white paper.
  2. Unfold it, and smooth it out a bit.
  3. Use a black marker to trace the crinkle lines in the paper.
  4. Now, use colored markers to fill in all the shapes you made with the black marker.

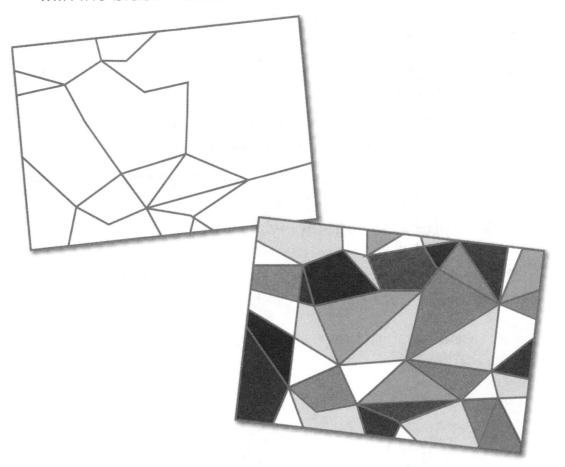

Duct Tape Wallet

Duct tape comes in lots of fun colors and patterns. You can use plain tape or something fancy for your wallet.

● **What You Need**

❏ duct tape

❏ scissors

❏ a ruler

❏ small hook-and-loop stickers

● **What You Do**

1. Cut out three strips of duct tape, each about 12 inches long.

2. Lay the pieces side by side, sticky side up. Stick them together, overlapping the edges just a little.

3. Cut out three more strips of tape, also 12 inches long.

4. Place these strips on top of the other pieces of tape, sticky side together.

5. Trim the ends on both sides so that they are even.

6. Fold the duct tape sheet in thirds to make a wallet.

7. If you like, cut one end into a triangle shape to make a flap for your wallet.

8. Tape the sides together with more tape (or a different color of tape).

9. Add a hook-and-loop sticker to the flap and the spot where it touches the main body of the wallet.

All you need to do now is earn some money to fill up your snazzy new wallet!

Me Collage

What's on your mind? What are your favorite things? Make a collage that's all about you!

- **What You Need**
  - ❏ heavy paper, like cardstock or construction paper
  - ❏ old magazines and catalogs
  - ❏ a marker
  - ❏ a glue stick

- **What You Do**
  1. Draw a large, simple outline of your head. Or, write your name in large bubble letters. Your outline or name should fill up most of the page. Here is a sample of what your head outline might look like.

  2. Look through the magazines and catalogs to find pictures of things you like or things that describe you. You might cut out pictures of your favorite animal, food, sport, color, or hobby. You can also look for words that describe you (silly, joyful, stubborn, musical, wild, shy) or things you like (green, cats, bikes, dinosaurs, ice cream, books, soccer).

  3. Cut out the pictures and words you like. Look for good places to fit them in on your collage.

  4. Once everything is where you want it, glue it in place.

Display your collage where your family can see it and learn more about the one and only you!

This type of collage makes a great gift. Make one for a parent or friend that shows just how well you know them.

Bean Mosaic

Beans are tasty to eat, but they can make a beautiful mosaic, too!

● **What You Need**

❏ a piece of cardboard (you can cut one from the side of a cereal box)

❏ glue

❏ a paintbrush

❏ a pencil

❏ dried beans in different colors

Note: If you don't have dried beans, you can use different types of dry cereal, but your mosaic may not last quite as long.

● **What You Do**

1. Begin by drawing a large, simple picture on the blank side of the cardboard. You might draw a tree and a sun, a flower, an apple, a butterfly, a kite, a fish, a snake, or a leaf.

2. Choose one area of your picture to work on. Squeeze glue on that area, and spread it out with the paintbrush. You'll need to apply it fairly thickly.

3. Glue the beans onto that area. Then, continue with the next area.

4. When your mosaic is done, give it plenty of time to dry. A piece or two may fall off— just re-glue them.

Stained Glass Butterfly

Create your own rare and beautiful butterfly! Hang it in the window to see a colorful stained glass design.

● **What You Need**

- ❏ 12-inch by 18-inch black construction paper
- ❏ tissue paper in assorted colors
- ❏ pencil
- ❏ scissors
- ❏ glue
- ❏ string or yarn
- ❏ paper hole punch

● **What You Do**

1. Fold the black paper in half lengthwise.

2. Draw half an outline of a butterfly.

3. Repeat the outline 1 inch inside the first outline, as shown. Leave space between the outlines.

4. With the design still folded in half, cut out the outline and inside of the shapes. Leave the borders uncut.

5. Unfold the butterfly and cut tissue paper to cover each opening. Make the tissue paper slightly larger than the opening.

6. Glue the tissue paper to the back of the butterfly covering each opening.

7. Punch a hole near the top and tie on a string.

8. Hang the butterfly from the ceiling or in a window.

Fill in the Faces

Fill in the face outlines below. Get creative and add anything you like—an extra eye, a hair bow, an enormous nose, a necktie, or antenna. Let your imagination run wild!

Foil Sculpture

Have you ever played with a piece of tinfoil? It's easy to bend and shape. That makes it a perfect material for sculpting!

- **What You Need**
  - ☐ tinfoil
  - ☐ a piece of cardboard
  - ☐ glue
  - ☐ newspaper (optional)

- **What You Do**

  1. Think about figures you would like to sculpt. Start with something simple. You could make an animal (like a dolphin, an octopus, a duck, or a snake), or you could make another simple object, like a boat, a tree, a cup, or a plane. Experiment a little until you get the hang of sculpting with foil.

  2. If you like, you can start off with crumpled newspaper as a base for your sculpture. You can also make your sculpture of just foil. Don't try to add too many details. And if you need to make small parts, like a tail or a stem, tear off a piece of foil, shape it, and press it back into the body of the object.

  3. When you're done, glue your sculpture to a piece of cardboard to display it.

If you like, you can paint your sculpture to give it a more finished look.

Another idea is to cover your sculpture with papier-mâché. Just cut up some paper into strips. Dip the strips in a mixture of water and glue. Smooth them onto your sculpture one piece at a time.

Window Clings

Add some glitter to the glue mixture to make sparkling window clings!

● **What You Need**

- ❏ white glue
- ❏ wax paper
- ❏ food coloring
- ❏ a sheet of paper
- ❏ tape
- ❏ a black pen or marker
- ❏ a small dish (optional)
- ❏ a paintbrush (optional)

● **What You Do**

1. On the paper, make several small pictures or designs with the marker. If it is winter, you can make snowflakes. If it is close to Valentine's Day, you can make hearts. Some other easy ideas are shamrocks, birds, stars, balloons, kites, and flowers.

2. Place a piece of wax paper over your drawings. If you need to, tape it down so you can see the designs well.

3. Decide what color you want to make your glue. If your bottle of glue is less than half full, just use the bottle. If it is fuller, pour about half the glue into a small dish.

4. Squeeze about 10 drops of food coloring into the glue. Put the lid on and shake the bottle, or stir the glue in the dish to mix it.

5. Squeeze (or paint) glue over your designs. Apply the glue thickly. There should be no empty spots.

6. Let the glue dry overnight. In the morning, you will have clings that are ready to stick to the windows!

Chinese Lantern

Chinese New Year is in late January or early February each year. Join the celebration by making this festive red lantern.

- **What You Need**
  - ❏ red construction paper
  - ❏ scissors
  - ❏ glue
  - ❏ ribbon or yarn
  - ❏ glitter glue (optional)

- **What You Do**
  1. Fold the construction paper in half lengthwise.
  2. Cut from the fold towards the edge of the paper. Do not cut all the way through—stop about an inch from the edge.
  3. Continue making cuts the same way (about an inch apart) all the way down the length of the paper.
  4. If you are using glitter glue, you can spread some lightly along the strips now.
  5. Once the glitter glue dries, make a tube of the paper so that the two shorter sides meet. Overlap the edges slightly, and glue them together. (You can also use double-stick tape.)
  6. After the glue dries, push down gently to make the lantern bend at the fold.
  7. Poke a small hole through the top of the lantern on either side. Thread a piece of ribbon or yarn through the holes, and tie it on both sides. This is the handle.

Your lantern is complete! If you have a **flameless** candle, you can place it inside the lantern to make it glow.

Design a Tee

Make a T-shirt that features your own artwork!

● **What You Need**

❏ a 100% cotton T-shirt in white or a light color

❏ crayons

❏ wax paper

❏ an iron

❏ an adult's help

● **What You Do**

1. Make sure you have a parent's permission to use the shirt.
2. Draw a picture or a design on the shirt.
3. Place a piece of wax paper over your design.
4. Have an adult iron the wax paper for about half a minute on the cotton setting.
5. Your shirt is done, and the design is permanent!

These T-shirts make a great gift. You can make ones with a theme for a friend (sports, horses, nature) or just draw a special picture for a parent or grandparent.

Yarn Stones

Go on a walk with a parent to see if you can find some stones to use for this project. If you can't find any, you can buy some at a craft store or a dollar store.

● **What You Need**

- ❏ yarn in different colors
- ❏ glue
- ❏ a small paintbrush
- ❏ smooth stones in different sizes

● **What You Do**

1. Cut several pieces of yarn in different colors.

2. Use the paintbrush to spread glue on half of one stone.

3. Start in the middle and tightly wrap yarn around the stone. Continue until you get to one end.

4. Go back to the middle and wrap the yarn to the other end. You may need to gently press down to make sure the yarn stays in place.

5. Make a whole set of yarn-covered stones. They make a beautiful decoration stacked or displayed in a little bowl.

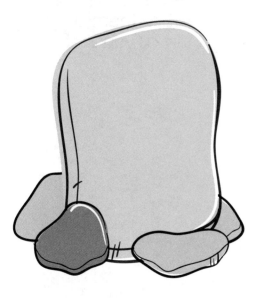

Tin Can Robots

Make a whole family of mix-and-match robots!

● **What You Need**

- ❏ one or more clean, empty cans (soup cans work well)
- ❏ small, plain magnets
- ❏ glue
- ❏ buttons, nuts and bolts, pipe cleaners, milk caps, bottle lids, pieces of craft foam, and so on

● **What You Do**

1. Peel the label off the soup can. (Watch out for any sharp edges at the open end of the can!)
2. Glue different items onto the magnets. Try to think what might work well for eyes, a nose, a mouth, ears, and hair for your robot.
3. Give the glue time to dry.
4. Decorate your robot. If you have more than one can, you can make several robots. Switch around the features to make new robots. Make them as goofy and silly as you like!

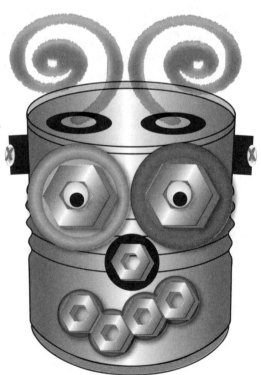

Flying Disc

Did you know that you can make a flying disc that works as well as one from the store? Just be sure not to use yours in wet weather!

● **What You Need**

❏ two paper plates

❏ scissors

❏ markers

❏ glue

❏ stickers (optional)

● **What You Do**

1. Cut out the inner circles of both paper plates.

2. Decorate the back side of both rings (not the side of the plates you would eat from). You can use markers and stickers to make your designs.

3. Glue the rims of the rings together. Your plates should look like this:

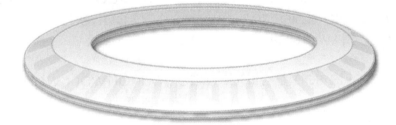

4. Once the glue has dried, you're ready to head outside and try it out!

Spaghetti Art

Spaghetti makes a great dinner. But it can also make a great piece of art!

● **What You Need**

☐ a piece of cardstock or thin cardboard

☐ cold cooked spaghetti

☐ glue

☐ a plastic cup

☐ paint

☐ paintbrushes

● **What You Do**

1. Pour some glue into the plastic cup. Mix in a little water to thin it.

2. Dip one piece of spaghetti at a time into the glue mixture.

3. Arrange the spaghetti on the cardstock (or cardboard) to make a picture or design.

4. Once your design is mostly dry, you can paint over it. If you use a single color, the shapes and pattern made by the spaghetti will really stand out.

If you like, sprinkle some glitter onto your artwork while the paint is still wet.

Flower Petal Bookmarks

These pretty bookmarks are handy to have around. Keep one in your room and one in your backpack.

- **What You Need**
  - ❏ a piece of cardstock (colored is fine)
  - ❏ flower petals or other small, natural bits
  - ❏ a piece of clear sticky paper (like contact paper) or clear packing tape
  - ❏ scissors
  - ❏ a ruler
  - ❏ a single-hole punch
  - ❏ a piece of ribbon

- **What You Do**
  1. Cut out a piece of cardstock about 6 inches long and 1½ inches wide.
  2. Arrange your flower petals on the cardstock.
  3. Carefully place the clear sticky paper or packing tape over the top of the bookmark.
  4. Smooth it down to get rid of any bubbles.
  5. Trim extra tape or sticky paper off the edges of the bookmark.
  6. Punch a hole in the center of the bookmark at the top.
  7. Thread a piece of ribbon through the hole and tie it in a knot.

Find a book and get busy reading—your bookmark is ready for action!

Easy Pom-Poms

Once you get the hang of making these cute pom-poms, you won't want to stop!

● **What You Need**

- ❏ yarn
- ❏ scissors
- ❏ a fork

● **What You Do**

1. Wind yarn around the tines of the fork. You'll need to do this about 50–75 times (depends on the type of yarn you use).

2. When you are done winding, take a small piece of yarn and tie it tightly around the center of the yarn like this.

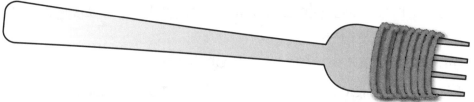

3. Slip the yarn bundle off the fork.

4. Cut through the loops on either side of the tie in the middle.

5. Fluff up the pom-pom, and trim off any uneven ends. You should end up with a nice, round ball.

Once you get the hang of this craft, you can make as many pom-poms as you like. String them together to make a pretty garland.

You can also try making little creatures. Glue two pom-poms together to make a bunny. Add ears made from felt and two googly eyes. Glue together five or six pom-poms to make a caterpillar, and add a couple of pipe cleaner antennas. Use your imagination!

Solve It

Crack the Code

Use the secret code to unlock the answer to a joke.

Why can't you play basketball with pigs?

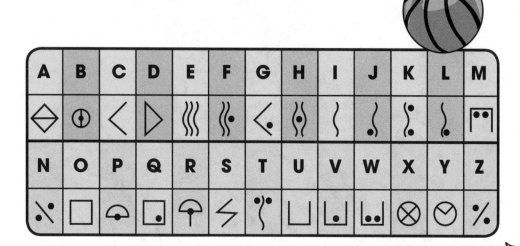

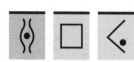

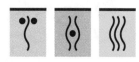

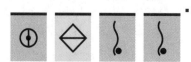

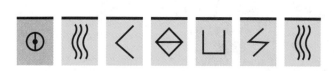

Sudoku Challenge

Complete the sudoku puzzle. Every row and column must contain the numbers **5**, **6**, **7**, and **8**. Do not repeat the same number twice in any row or column.

5			7
	8	6	
	5	7	
6			8

Crossword Opposites

Write the correct opposite into the crossword.

● **Across**

    1. opposite of new

    2. _____ is the opposite of loud.

    5. opposite of up

    6. If something is small, it is not _____.

● **Down**

    1. _____ is the opposite of in.

    3. opposite of over

    4. If you are _____ then you are not near.

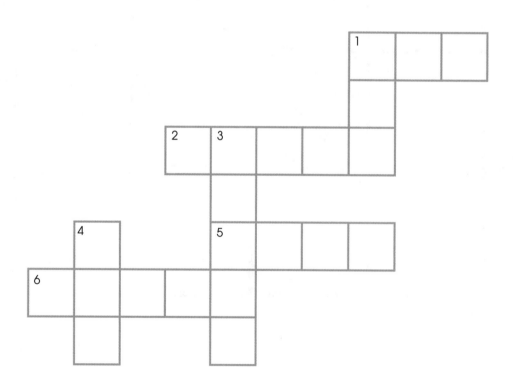

Journey to the Pyramids

Help the dog visit the Pyramids of Giza.

Start

Finish

Secret Code

Decode the message using the symbols below.

A	B	C	D	E	F	G	H	I	J	K	L	M

N	O	P	Q	R	S	T	U	V	W	X	Y	Z

What a Great Place!

Fill in the puzzle with words that name the pictures below. Use the word box to help you.

1.
2.
3.
4.
5.
6.

teacher
pencil
book
crayons
eraser
chalk

The letters in the circles going down spell a mystery word. The word names a place where all these things can be found.

Write the mystery word.

_____

Going Places

Read the clues and use the words in the word box to complete the puzzle.

● **Across**

1. It is an automobile.
4. Hot air makes it rise into the sky.
6. This can carry heavy loads on the road.

● **Down**

2. This flies people from city to city.
3. This carries people and big loads on water.
4. It has two wheels and pedals.
5. This takes many people around the city.

airplane
bike
bus
car
truck
boat
balloon

Winter Treat

Hop the marshmallows to the hot cocoa.

Start

Finish

Crack the Code

Use the secret code to discover a silly but true fact.

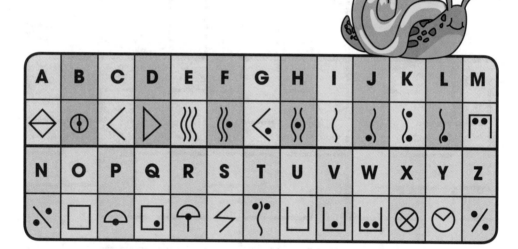

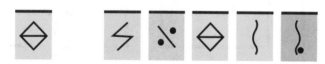

Word Scramble

Look at the pictures and words. The words are all scrambled up!
Write the word correctly on the lines.

mclea _____

bltae _____

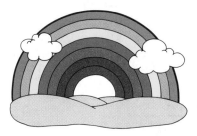

wrinoab _____

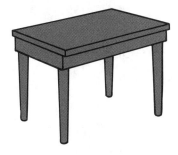

ttrebyulf _____

ovclona _____

Name:

Firefighters

Read the clues and use the words in the word box to complete the puzzle.

● **Across**

3. They put on their _____ , boots, and helmets.

5. As the fire alarm goes off, the firefighters _____ down the nearest fire pole.

6. They jump onto the fire _____ .

● **Down**

1. They check, _____ , and put away all of their equipment.

2. After the fire is put out, the firefighters go back to the fire _____ .

4. They turn on their siren and speed away to _____ the fire.

engine
slide
house
fight
clean
coats

Sudoku Challenge

Complete the sudoku puzzle. Every row and column must contain the numbers **1**, **2**, **3**, and **4**. Do not repeat the same number twice in any row or column.

1			3
	4	2	
	1	3	
2			4

Magic Number 16

Connect as many pairs as you can to make the sum.

Sum of 16

Solve It

TECH Timeout

Grade 2

Crack the Code

Use the secret code to unlock the answer to a joke.

Why was the baby ant confused?

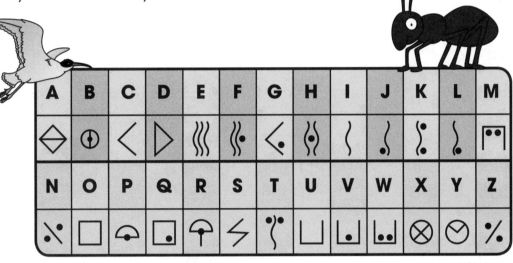

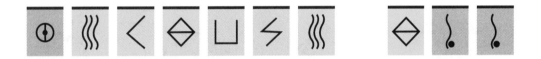

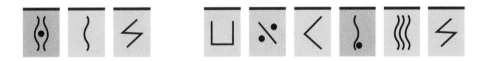

Loose Change

A little boy asks for your help. He put six coins in his pocket, and they all fell out! The coins add up to 95 cents. Can you help the boy find them?

Look at the coins below. Decide which coins were in the boy's pocket.

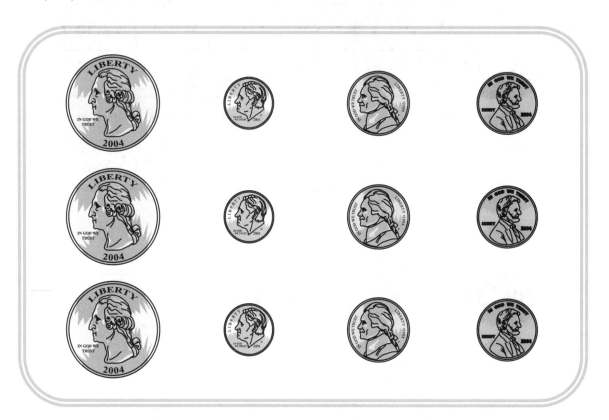

Suppose the boy had a different set of coins that added up to 95 cents. Draw what he might have had.

Sweet Spring

Read the clues and use the words in the word box to complete the puzzle.

● **Across**

   2. It is the opposite of colder.

   3. These bloom in the spring.

   6. You can fly one outdoors in the spring.

   7. Take your umbrella on days like this.

● **Down**

   1. This is busy eating new leaves in spring.

   4. It's fun to play here.

   5. This is a good day to fly a kite.

warmer
flowers
caterpillar
windy
rainy
kite
outdoors

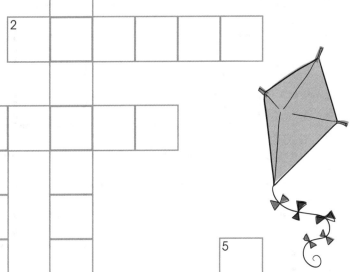

Play Ball!

Help the pup fetch her ball.

Start

Finish

A Taste of Italy

Unscramble the letters to spell three different toppings on each pizza.

onpepiper

mah

oomsshmur

mushrooms
green peppers
ground beef
ham
sausage
onions
olives
spinach
pepperoni

_____

_____

_____

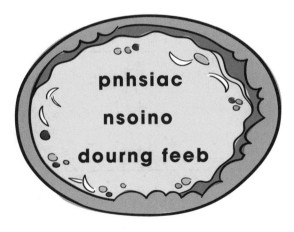

pnhsiac

nsoino

dourng feeb

vslieo

gseauas

energ prseepp

_____

_____

_____

_____

_____

_____

Grade 2 TECH Timeout Solve It 85

Presto!

Exchange one letter from each pair of words to make two new words.

Example: **l**ost — **p**ace becomes **p**ost — **l**ace.

Hint: The letter will not always be the first letter of each word.

hat — point   _____ — _____

meat — nail   _____ — _____

brain — get   _____ — _____

like — bat   _____ — _____

dear — way   _____ — _____

Springtime Puzzler

Use the word lists to fill out the grid below.

Hint: Count the squares in the grid first to see where the words will fit.

3 Letters	4 Letters	5 Letters	6 Letters
sun	root	bloom	flower
May	warm	green	energy
	buds	slush	
	rain		

Hippopotamus Words

How many words can you make from the letters in **HIPPOPOTAMUS**?

MUST   TAP

Snack Attack

Read the clues and use the words in the word box to complete the puzzle.

● **Across**

    3. It comes from cows.

    5. It can go in a pie.

    7. It is good with jelly.

● **Down**

    1. It is brown and sweet.

    2. Rabbits like them.

    4. It is made from milk.

    6. It can be red, yellow, or green.

    8. It is yellow and grows in a bunch.

apple
cherry
peanut butter
raisin
cheese
milk
carrots
banana

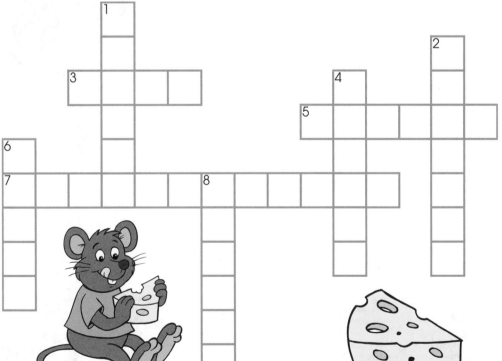

Unscramble Time

Unscramble each word. Be sure it goes with the meaning.

1. One who plays is called a

   lapeyr   ___ ___ ___ ___ ___ ___.

2. A round thing you can kick is a

   lalb   ___ ___ ___ ___.

3. A sweet treat to eat is

   danyc   ___ ___ ___ ___ ___.

4. Something you can win is a

   pzire   ___ ___ ___ ___ ___.

5. A person who wins is the

   rnnewi   ___ ___ ___ ___ ___ ___.

6. One who sails a boat is a

   ailsor   ___ ___ ___ ___ ___ ___.

| prize | winner | player | ball | sailor | candy |

Race to the Finish Line

Help the racer reach the finish line.

Start

Finish

Four Square

Starting with the top word in each square, change one letter at a time until the top word becomes the bottom word.

1.	B	O	N	E
2.				
3.				
4.				
5.	C	A	P	S

6.	T	A	L	K
7.				
8.				
9.				
10.	D	I	M	E

Animal Homes

Read the clues and use the words in the word box to complete the puzzle.

● **Across**

    3. This is where bees make their honey.

    4. This is a home for a clam.

    6. Fish and frogs live here.

    7. A bird makes this home.

● **Down**

    1. Ants build one to live in.

    2. This is where a spider lives.

    5. A beaver builds a dam near this home.

    8. A hole in this makes a good home for a squirrel.

web
tree
nest
lodge
hive
hill
shell
pond

Time to Rhyme

Use the picture clues to match the rhyming words.

1.  meat

2.  seal

3. king

4. mouse

5. clock

6. hair

7.  dog

8.  boat

 sock

 wheel

 bear

 ring

 goat

 frog

 feet

 house

Compound Fun

Match each word in the word box with a word in the puzzle to make a new word.

| cake | shine | knob | room |
| port | shore | ball | fish |

1. | s | e | a | | | | |

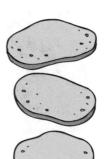

2. | a | i | r | | | |

3. | p | a | n | | | |

4. | s | u | n | | | |

5. | d | o | o | r | | | |

6. | b | a | t | h | | | |

7. | f | o | o | t | | | |

8. | g | o | l | d | | | |

Word Scramble

Look at the pictures and words. The words are all scrambled up!
Write the word correctly on the lines.

linsa _____

letrut _____

onstrme _____

yonemk _____

ruqrtea _____

Sudoku Challenge

Complete the sudoku puzzle. Every row and column must contain the numbers **1**, **2**, **3**, and **4**. Do not repeat the same number twice in any row or column.

	4	2	1
2	1	4	

Crack the Code

Use the secret code to unlock the answer to a joke.

Why did the banana go to the doctor?

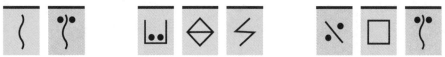

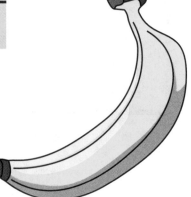

Halloween Fun

Read the clues and use the words in the word box to complete the puzzle.

● **Across**

  2. Placed over your face

  6. Carved pumpkin

  7. Halloween month

● **Down**

  1. Dracula is one of these.

  3. Stirs potions in a cauldron

  4. A house where ghosts live is considered _____.

  5. Disguise

October
mask
jackolantern
costume
witch
haunted
vampire

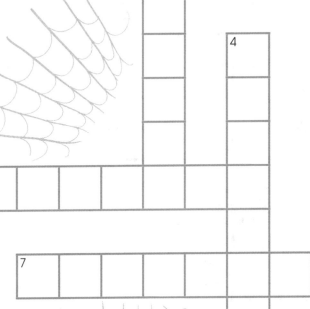

Head Hunter

Help the cat visit the Moai.

Finish

Start

Secret Code

Write the letter for each symbol. Use the code at the bottom of the page.

What happened when the Easter Bunny told a bunch of silly jokes?

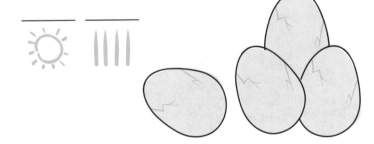

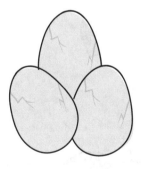

L	A	F	O	E	T	H	G

S	C	K	R	D	P	U

Busy Year

Use the word lists to fill out the grid below.

Hint: Count the squares in the grid first to see where the words will fit.

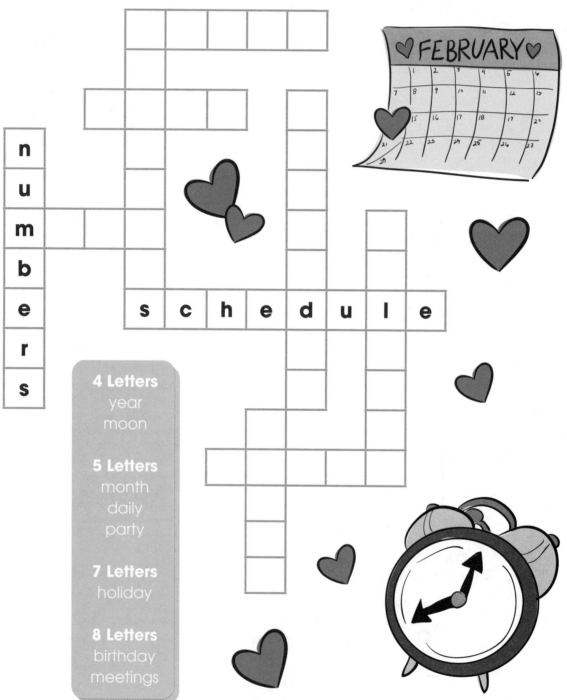

4 Letters
year
moon

5 Letters
month
daily
party

7 Letters
holiday

8 Letters
birthday
meetings

Sunshine Words

How many words can you make from the letters in **SUNSHINE**?

SUN   HIS

Riddle Time

Use the word box on the next page to answer each clue in the squares on the right. Then, use your answers to fill in the letters of the riddle on the next page.

a. Not old

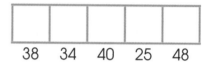

38 34 40 25 48

b. _____ and thank you

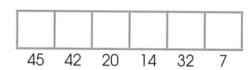

45 42 20 14 32 7

c. Police _____

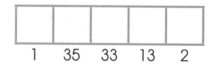

41 9 24 4 46 11 15

d. Tells the time

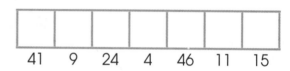

1 35 33 13 2

e. You smell with this

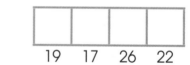

19 17 26 22

f. Long stream of water

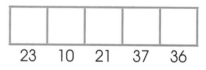

23 10 21 37 36

g. Female nobility

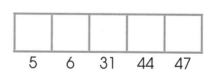

5 6 31 44 47

h. What you do with a paddle

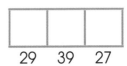

29	39	27

i. Japanese currency

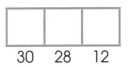

30	28	12

j. You don't _____? (rhymes with "hay")

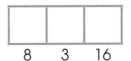

8	3	16

k. Second and last vowels in the alphabet, not including "y"

43	18

watch   please
river   EU
yen   nose
young   station
queen   say
row

$\overline{}\ \overline{}\ \overline{}\ \overline{}$ $\overline{}\ \overline{}\ \overline{}\ \overline{}\ \overline{}\ \overline{}\ \overline{}\ \overline{}$ $\overline{}\ \overline{}\ \overline{}$
1   2   3   4   5   6   7   8   9 10 11 12   13 14 15

16 17 18   19 20 21 22 23   24 25 26 27 28 29

" _____ _____ _____ " _____ _____ ?
30 31 32   33 34

" _____ _____ _____   _____ _____ _____   _____ _____ _____ _____ _____ _____ _____ _____ ? "
35 36 37   38 39 40   41 42 43 44 45 46 47 48

Nursery Rhymes

Read the clues and use the words in the word box to complete the puzzle.

● **Across**

2. Jack and Jill went up the _____.
4. One, two, buckle my _____.
7. Little Jack Horner sat in the _____.

● **Down**

1. Hey diddle, diddle,
   the cat and the _____.
3. Mary had a little _____.
4. Little Bo-peep has lost her _____.
5. Hickory, dickory, dock,
   the mouse ran up the _____.
6. Little Boy Blue,
   come blow your _____.

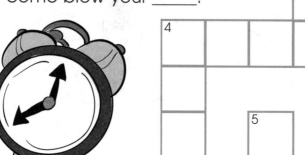

clock
lamb
hill
sheep
shoe
fiddle
horn
corner

Trotting Right Along

Trot the pony to the giant carrot.

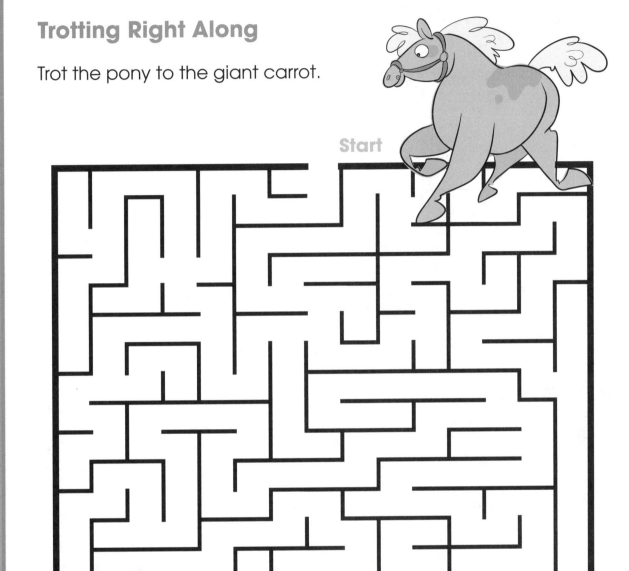

Start

Finish

Spa Party!

Unscramble the words and write them on the lines.

nrmeacui __ __ __ __ __ __ __ __

varkmeoe __ __ __ __ __ __ __ __

deipurce __ __ __ __ __ __ __ __

filaca __ __ __ __ __ __

smasega __ __ __ __ __ __ __

facial
massage
makeover
pedicure
manicure

Award Shows

Write the missing letters **a**, **c**, **e**, **n**, or **o** for each word. Use the code at the bottom of the page.

__ s __ __ r s

__ __ __ d __ m y

H __ l l y w __ __ d

w i __ __ __ r

r __ d __ __ r p __ t

A	C	E	N	O
☆	☺	♡	✳	▨

At the Pool

Use the word lists to fill out the grid below.

Hint: Count the squares in the grid first to see where the words will fit.

3 Letters	4 Letters	5 Letters	6 Letters	7 Letters
tan	pool	slide	lotion	whistle
sun	dive	float		
	raft			
	rest			
	laps			

Facing the Sun

Read the clues and use the words in the word box to complete the puzzle.

● **Across**

1. A farm animal.
2. A buzzing bug.
4. A fruit.
6. A very tall plant.
7. The color of grass.
8. A big bird.

● **Down**

1. At night you _____.
3. A mouse eats _____.
5. You _____ food.
6. 2 + 1 = _____.
9. A part of a plant.

bee
cheese
eat
sheep
green
peach
tree
sleep
eagle
leaf
three

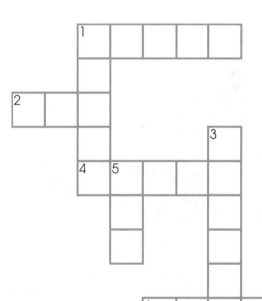

Surprise Code!

Use the key to figure out the code and unscramble the answer to the question.

What has two heads, twenty-four legs and sharp, pointy teeth?

KEY	
A	1
B	2
D	3
G	4
H	5
I	6
K	7
N	8
O	9
R	10
S	11
T	12
U	13
W	14
Y	15

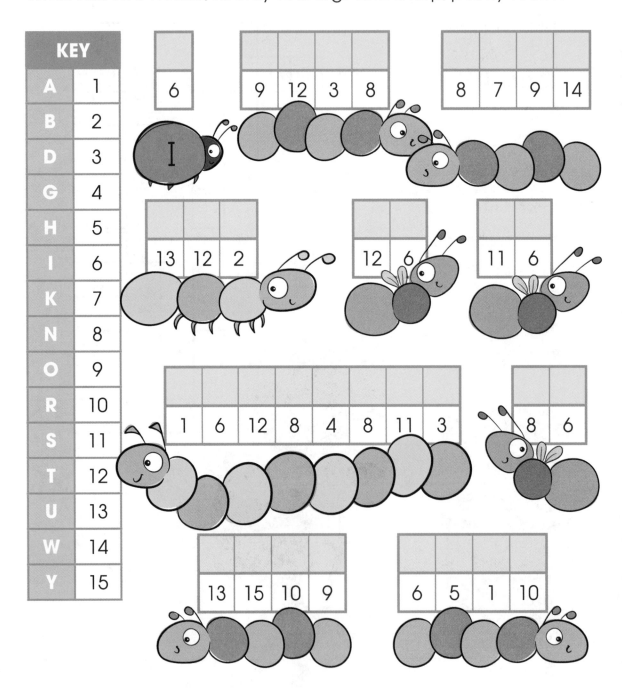

6

9 12 3 8

8 7 9 14

13 12 2

12 6

11 6

1 6 12 8 4 8 11 3

8 6

13 15 10 9

6 5 1 10

Shape Sudoku

Complete the sudoku puzzle. Every row and column must contain a △, ●, ♥, and ☐. Do not repeat the same shape twice in any row or column.

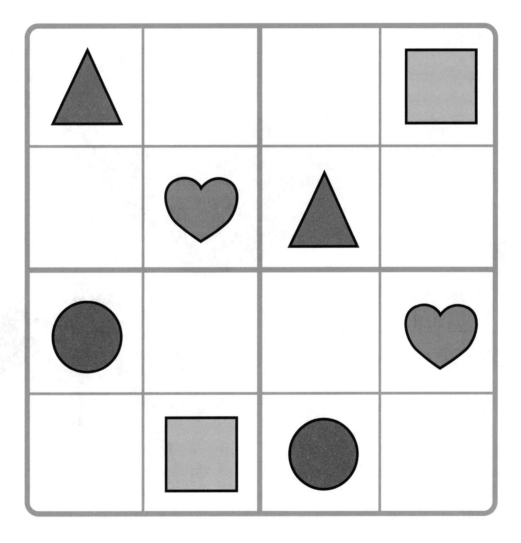

Slumber Party!

Write the missing letters **a**, **e**, **g**, **o**, **m**, or **s** for each word. Use the code at the bottom of the page.

p i l l __ w   f i __ h t

__ __ __ __ i p
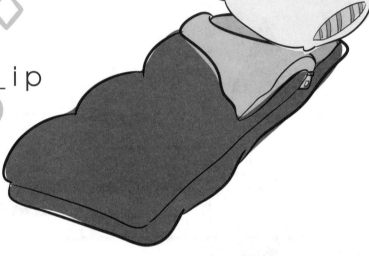

d __ n c __

__ __ v i __ __

__ __ k __ o v __ r s

A	E	G	O	M	S

To the Top of the Needle

Help the dog visit the Seattle Space Needle.

U.S.A.

Start

Finish

Wild West

Use the word lists to fill out the grid below.

Hint: Count the squares in the grid first to see where the words will fit.

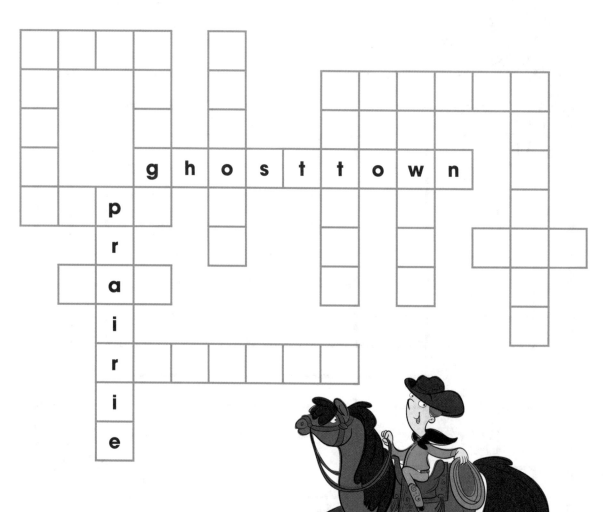

3 Letters	4 Letters	5 Letters	6 Letters	7 Letters
map	pipe	range	cowboy	sheriff
aim	spur	sheep	cactus	rawhide
			cattle	
			saloon	

Calendar Crossword

Read the clues and use the words in the word box to complete the puzzle.

● **Across**

    2. It is a day for celebrating instead of working.

    3. It can be measured in days, weeks, months, and years.

    4. It can have 28 to 31 days.

    6. You can hang it on a wall to keep track of the days.

    8. This has twelve months.

● **Down**

    1. This is the day you were born.

    5. It has seven days.

    7. A year has 365 of these.

days
week
month
year
calendar
holiday
birthday
time

Pig Pen Puzzler

Use the word box on the next page to answer each clue in the squares on the right. Then, use your answers to fill in the letters of the riddle on the next page.

a. Makes you say, "Ouch!"

8	3	9	12

b. Class where you learn to add

25	11	4	32

c. Where bees live

17	14	19	41

d. Hospital room with a TV and magazines

1	7	21	31	34	42	10

e. You bake in it

30	35	20	22

f. Piggy _____

29	18	38	16

g. Swimming place

40	24	27	33

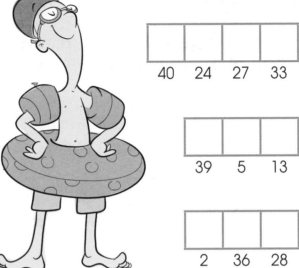

h. Opposite of "subtract"

39	5	13

i. It lays eggs

2	36	28

j. A penny is a _____

23	6	37	15

k. Thirteenth letter of the alphabet

26

coin   hen
hive   math
bank   M
pain   add
pool   waiting
oven

| 1 | 2 | 3 | 4 | | 5 | 6 | | 7 | | 8 | 9 | 10 | | 11 | 12 | 13 |

?

| 14 | 15 | 16 | | 17 | 18 | 19 | 20 | | 21 | 22 | | 23 | 24 | 25 | 26 | 27 | 28 |

| 29 | 30 | 31 | 32 | | 33 | 34 | 35 | 36 | | 37 | 38 | | 39 | | 40 | 41 | 42 |

World Traveler

Write the missing letters **a**, **d**, **e**, **n**, or **y** for each word. Use the code at the bottom of the page.

__ __ g l __ __ __
♡ ✿ ☺ ✿ ☆

G __ r m __ __ __
♡ ☺ ✿ 〰

F i __ l __ __ __
✿ ☺ ✿ ☆

J __ p __ __
☺ ☺ ✿

I t __ l __
☺ 〰

A	D	E	N	Y
☺	☆	♡	✿	〰

A-Maze-ing Alien

Help the alien find his ride.

MAYBE HE CAN GIVE ME A LIFT HOME!

Start

Finish

Found in Space

Read each riddle. Then, write the answer using one of the scrambled words from the word box.

1. This huge star lights the day. ___ ___ ___

2. These shine at night. ___ ___ ___ ___ ___

3. These are on the Moon. ___ ___ ___ ___ ___ ___ ___

4. This is our home planet. ___ ___ ___ ___ ___

5. This flies into space. ___ ___ ___ ___ ___ ___ ___

6. This planet is red. ___ ___ ___ ___

7. This planet has rings. ___ ___ ___ ___ ___ ___

8. Astronauts do this in space. ___ ___ ___ ___ ___

tlfoa
nuS
htlesut
srast
rEath
nruSat
rMas
erscrat

Slumbering Slippers

Read the clues and use the words in the word box to complete the puzzle.

● **Across**

4. Opposite of frown.

5. A small, slow-moving creature.

6. Opposite of rough.

9. Resting.

10. To slant or lean.

11. What your nose does.

13. Intelligent.

14. Ah . . . choo!

● **Down**

1. To shut with a bang.

2. A smooth, layered rock.

3. A cracking sound.

4. Very clever, like a fox.

6. To trip.

7. A kind of shoe.

8. Reptiles.

11. Frozen white flakes.

12. Something burning gives off.

smooth	snail	sly
slam	smart	slip
slipper	snow	smile
slope	slate	smoke
snakes	smells	sneeze
snap	sleeping	

Who's at the Zoo?

Use the word lists to fill out the grid below.

Hint: Count the squares in the grid first to see where the words will fit.

	3 Letters	4 Letters	5 Letters	6 Letters	7 Letters	8 Letters
	cub	cage	tiger	snakes	habitat	elephant
	pet	deer	teeth	safari	peanuts	

Castle Quest

Get the queen to her castle.

CASTLES ARE OK, BUT I LIKE THE CROWN!

Start

Finish

Sea Turtle Words

How many words can you make from the letters in **SEA TURTLES**?

EAR

_____

_____

_____

_____

_____

_____

_____

RAT

_____

_____

_____

_____

_____

_____

_____

Holiday Crossword

Write the holidays from the word box in the puzzle. Then, find the secret word in the purple box.

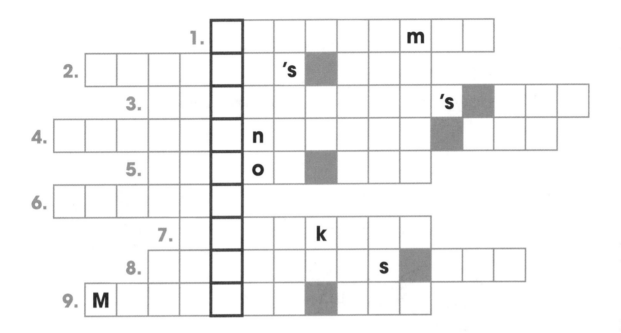

The secret word is _____.

Mother's Day   Independence Day   Easter
Father's Day   Arbor Day   Valentine's Day
Veterans Day   Christmas   Hanukkah

Land and Water

Read the clues and use the words in the word box to complete the puzzle.

● **Across**

2. This is a body of fresh water surrounded by land.
4. This is a very high hill.
6. This is low land between mountains or hills.

● **Down**

1. This is a very flat stretch of land.
3. This is a flowing stream of water.
5. This is a large body of salt water.

valley
plain
mountain
ocean
lake
river

Surf's Up!

Help the surfer catch some waves.

Start

Finish

Beaver Clues

Use the word box to answer each clue in the squares. Then, use your answers to fill in the letters of the riddle on the next page.

a. Lima _____

11	35	32	43

b. To be patient

45	3	6	8

c. Used to chew food

22	41	24	25	2

d. Season

1	39	37	4	12	26

e. Stringed instrument

42	51	29	20	13	16

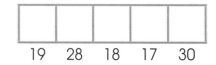

f. Makes bread rise

19	28	18	17	30

winter	heady	dogs
bean	guitar	yeast
chin	bee	oven
H	wait	teeth

g. Wanting one's own way

9	15	44	5	49

h. It's below your lips

40	31	46	38

i. Baking appliance

50	14	10	47

j. It's raining cats and _____

7	21	48	33

k. What insect makes honey?

34	27	36

l. Eighth letter of the alphabet

23

___ ___ ___ ___   ___ ___ ___   ___ ___ ___   ___ ___ ___ ___ ___ ___
1   2   3   4   5   6   7   8   9   10   11 12 13 14 15 16

___ ___ ___   ___ ___   ___ ___ ___   ___ ___ ___ ___ ?
17 18 19   20 21   22 23 24   25 26 27 28

___ ___   ___ ___ ___   ___ ___ ___ ___   ___ ___ ___ ___
29 30   31 32 33   34 35 36 37   38 39 40 41

___ ___ ___ ___ ___ ___ ___   ___ ___ ___ !
42 43 44 45 46 47 48   49 50 51

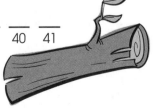

Kitten Family

How many words can you make from the letters in **KITTEN FAMILY**?

KITE   MAN

_____   _____

_____   _____

_____   _____

_____   _____

_____   _____

_____   _____

_____   _____

Summer Fun

Use the word lists to fill out the grid below.

Hint: Count the squares in the grid first to see where the words will fit.

3 Letters	4 Letters	5 Letters	6 Letters
hot	swim	skate	movies
tan	bike	storm	shorts
run	kite		
	sail		
	cone		

Hidden Message

The answer to the question below is hidden on pages in this book. Look at each page number. Turn to that page, and find the red letter. Write the letter on the line.

This bird migrates from the Arctic to Antarctica and back again each year. It migrates farther than any other kind of bird—about 25,000 miles! Which bird is it?

$$\overline{} \quad \overline{} \quad \overline{} \quad \overline{} \quad \overline{} \quad \overline{}$$
32   101   70   14   93   128

$$\overline{} \quad \overline{} \quad \overline{} \quad \overline{}$$
41   113   57   87

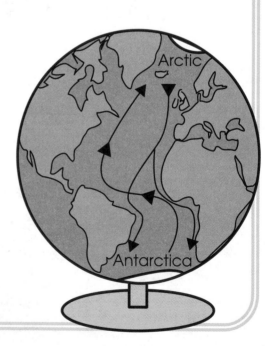

Arctic

Antarctica

Find It

The Wild West

Color the spaces with long vowel words **brown**. Color the spaces with short vowel words **blue**.

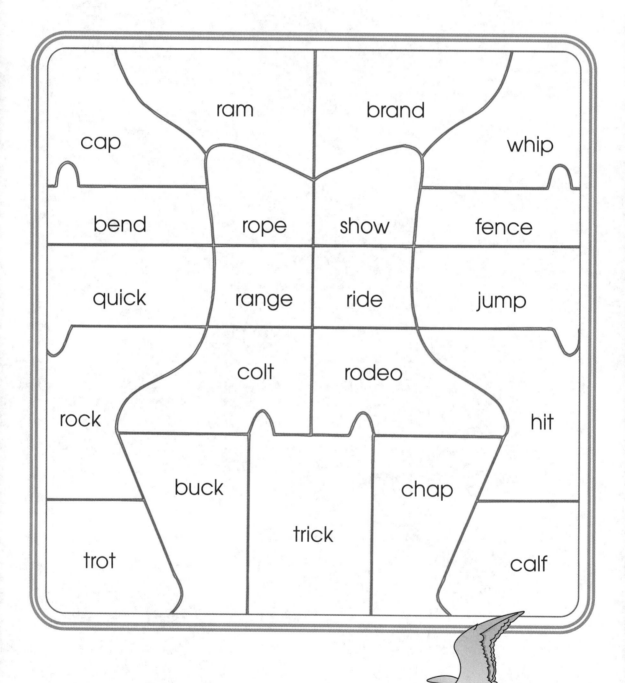

ram | brand
cap | whip
bend | rope | show | fence
quick | range | ride | jump
colt | rodeo
rock | hit
buck | chap
trick
trot | calf

What did you color? _____

Indoor Shape Hunt

Shapes are everywhere. You just have to look carefully to see them. Take a walk through your house to hunt for shapes. See if you can find each shape listed below. On the line, write where you found the shape.

❏ circle _____

❏ square _____

❏ triangle _____

❏ diamond _____

❏ oval _____

❏ straight line _____

❏ heart _____

❏ Z shape _____

❏ X shape _____

❏ W shape _____

❏ V shape _____

❏ U shape _____

❏ T shape _____

❏ S shape _____

Rainy Day Treasure Hunt

Find the 25 hidden items in the room next door.

- ❏ banana
- ❏ domino
- ❏ toothbrush
- ❏ cheese wedge
- ❏ pizza slice
- ❏ sock
- ❏ pine tree
- ❏ leaf
- ❏ marker
- ❏ mushroom
- ❏ horseshoe
- ❏ smiley face
- ❏ top hat
- ❏ paint can
- ❏ comb
- ❏ hockey stick
- ❏ heart
- ❏ lemon slice
- ❏ ruler
- ❏ lollipop
- ❏ ring
- ❏ crown
- ❏ soup can
- ❏ paintbrush
- ❏ sailboat

Nature Words

Find the nature words from the word box. Words can be across, down, diagonal, or backward.

flower	seeds	birds	rain
water cycle	insects	habitat	
soil	clouds	evaporation	

```
e  x  r  y  l  w  b  i  r  d  s  f
z  v  e  e  n  t  l  a  e  s  e  p
r  w  a  t  e  r  c  y  c  l  e  m
h  y  l  p  t  i  w  e  l  s  d  q
a  r  j  h  o  p  r  s  o  m  s  s
b  m  a  d  c  r  k  u  u  h  y  o
i  n  b  i  l  t  a  z  d  q  j  i
t  r  p  g  n  i  w  t  s  c  s  l
a  d  p  x  v  e  d  c  i  v  p  n
t  r  e  w  o  l  f  g  y  o  s  l
g  p  g  r  s  e  e  r  d  o  n  o
l  f  h  x  i  n  s  e  c  t  s  y
```

What Is It?

Color the spaces with words that name vehicles yellow. Color the other spaces blue.

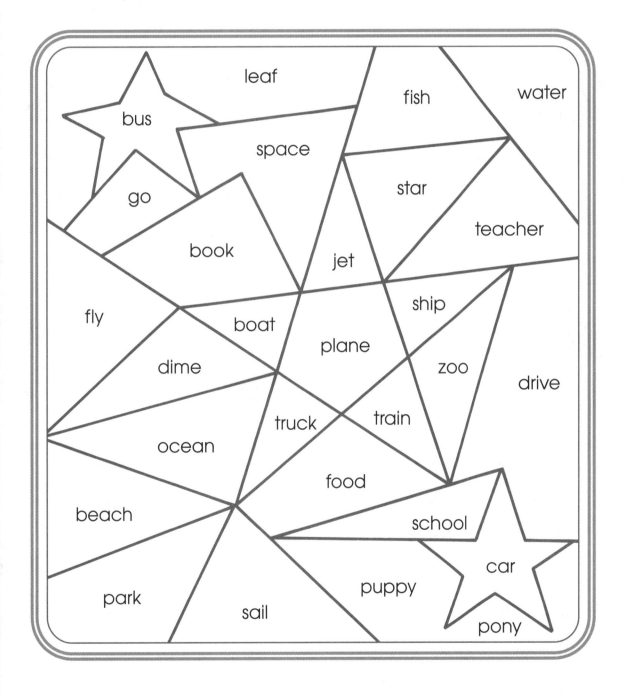

Kitchen Scavenger Hunt

Is it in the cupboard? Is it in the fridge? Maybe it is sitting right on the counter. Read the list of words below. For each word, find something in the kitchen that it describes. Write what you find on the line.

❏ sticky _____

❏ frozen _____

❏ sweet _____

❏ sharp _____

❏ shiny _____

❏ crunchy _____

❏ soft _____

❏ plastic _____

❏ metal _____

❏ wet _____

❏ fresh _____

❏ yellow _____

❏ tiny _____

❏ broken _____

❏ new _____

❏ striped _____

Tiny Dinos

Compsognathus was a tiny dinosaur that was no bigger than a chicken. Because it weighed about 5 pounds, Compsognathus was probably quick and light on its feet. It could chase down insects and other small animals, then use its sharp teeth and claws.

There are six of these tiny dinosaurs hiding in the picture below. Can you find them all? Circle each one.

People Scavenger Hunt

People watching can be fun. When you are in a crowded place, see if you can spot the people described below.

❏ wearing a green jacket

❏ with curly hair

❏ woman wearing a hat

❏ with a baby carrier

❏ with a mustache

❏ wearing stripes

❏ with a backpack

❏ reading a book

❏ wearing yellow

Magic Number 11

Circle the pairs that equal 11.

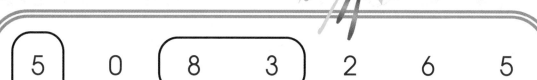

5	0	8	3	2	6	5
6	7	4	1	9	11	0
10	1	0	9	2	8	3
8	2	4	6	5	10	1
3	9	1	10	9	2	6
4	7	11	7	4	0	5
10	1	0	11	7	8	3

Nuts, Seeds, and Beans

Find and circle the words in the puzzle.

peanut				coconut
almond	pea	walnut	chestnut
soybean	pecan	macadamia	cashew
lima	pod	pistachio	shell

```
m  a  c  a  d  a  m  i  a  f  c  w
j  l  i  m  a  k  m  i  p  p  e  a
n  m  p  e  a  n  u  t  o  e  g  l
c  o  c  o  n  u  t  h  d  c  e  n
l  n  s  o  y  b  e  a  n  a  a  u
d  d  r  o  c  h  e  s  t  n  u  t
c  a  s  h  e  w  s  s  h  e  l  l
b  p  q  p  i  s  t  a  c  h  i  o
```

What's Different?

Can you spot the 10 differences in these two pictures?

Vehicle Scavenger Hunt

Next time you are riding in the car, keep your eyes on the road and watch for the vehicles shown below. Can you find them all? Check off each one as you see it.

❏ ambulance

❏ dump truck

❏ motorcycle

❏ bikes on a car

❏ delivery van

❏ semi truck

❏ white pick-up

❏ yellow car

❏ bus
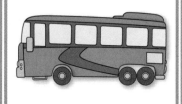

Shirts and Shoes

If you put **s** and **h** together, they make the **sh** sound. How many things can you find in this picture that begin with **sh**? Circle them.

shadow	shark	shelf	ship	shoes	shutters
shapes	sheep	shells	shirt	shop	

Write three more words that begin with **sh**.

_____ _____ _____

Magazine Scavenger Hunt

Find a bunch of old magazines. Be sure no one wants them anymore. Then, grab a pair of scissors and look at the list below.

Flip through the pages. When you find something from the list, cut out the picture. Glue or tape the picture in the box or on another sheet of paper.

Find . . .

- ❑ someone laughing
- ❑ the sun
- ❑ someone eating
- ❑ a boat
- ❑ water
- ❑ a white dog
- ❑ someone in a car
- ❑ a child with a toy
- ❑ grass
- ❑ someone using a phone

Shape Search

Find and circle the words in the puzzle.

circle	diamond	star
square	rectangle	heart
oval	octagon	sphere
triangle	hexagon	cube

```
x o c i r c l e l q t s a
o v h t r i a n g l e q c
c a s j r s p h e r e u r
t l e g i t b c n n e a s
a u h e x a g o n m a r c
g v h e a r t p c f w e p
o d n e p t a g o n w n n
n r e c t a n g l e x o t
c u b e z y d i a m o n d
```

Barnyard Treasure Hunt

Find the 28 hidden items in the barn next door.

- ❏ light bulb
- ❏ heart
- ❏ sock
- ❏ slice of bread
- ❏ spoon
- ❏ soup can
- ❏ umbrella
- ❏ mushroom
- ❏ sailboat
- ❏ snail
- ❏ flower pot
- ❏ pizza slice
- ❏ glove
- ❏ stamp
- ❏ toothbrush
- ❏ envelope
- ❏ fishhook
- ❏ crescent moon
- ❏ bell
- ❏ eyeglasses
- ❏ comb
- ❏ candle
- ❏ lollipop
- ❏ ice cream cone
- ❏ glass with straw
- ❏ needle
- ❏ ruler
- ❏ pencil

What's Different?

Can you spot the 10 differences in these two pictures?

Mystery Sentence

Color the following words in the puzzle **green**.

> if   is   but   shoe   can   house   in

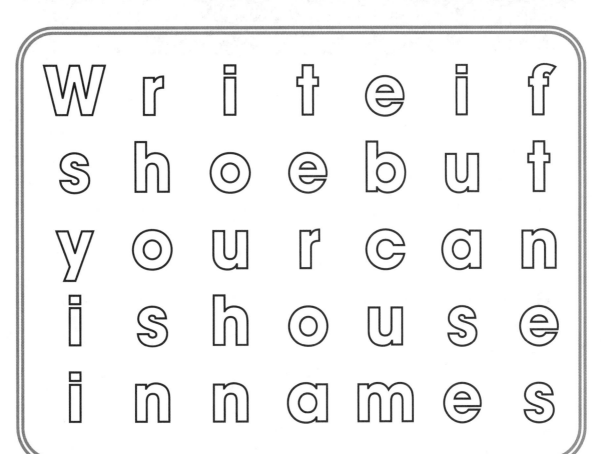

Write the words you did not color to make a sentence.

_____ _____ _____ .

Bicycle Words

Find and circle the words in the puzzle.

seat	pedal	tire	wheels
chain	spokes	light	horn
brakes	fenders	gears	frame
hub			reflector

```
f r a m e c h a i n n e
e c r j b p b f z t a h
n l k w g e r y s m g u
d i t h a d a o e f e b
e g i e s a k x a h a u
r h r e f l e c t o r p
s t e l c d s w i r s v
d q h s p o k e s n l b
```

Match the Dinosaurs

Pachycephalosaurus had a thick bone on the top of its head. Knobs and spikes stuck out from this dome and the dinosaur's nose. Pachycephalosaurus may have crashed heads with rival dinosaurs to become the leader of the herd or to win mates.

Circle the two pictures below that are exactly alike.

Dragon Treasure Hunt

Find the 23 hidden items in the scene next door.

- ❏ cherry
- ❏ butterfly
- ❏ paperclip
- ❏ golf club
- ❏ balloon
- ❏ mitten
- ❏ diamond
- ❏ pizza slice
- ❏ teacup
- ❏ candy corn
- ❏ heart
- ❏ megaphone
- ❏ glove
- ❏ stamp
- ❏ sock
- ❏ flower pot
- ❏ umbrella
- ❏ domino
- ❏ leaf
- ❏ flag
- ❏ sailboat
- ❏ banana
- ❏ party hat

Name:

Reptile Search

Find and circle the words in the puzzle.

turtle	tortoise	sidewinder
iguana	alligator	chameleon
crocodile	gecko	anaconda
lizard	skink	rattlesnake

```
a  r  a  t  t  l  e  s  n  a  k  e  c
l  c  r  o  c  o  d  i  l  e  z  a  h
l  t  o  r  t  o  i  s  e  l  i  n  a
i  d  u  w  x  a  k  j  g  i  g  a  m
g  e  y  r  v  o  l  n  e  z  u  c  e
a  t  s  u  t  p  m  g  c  a  a  o  l
t  c  b  r  q  l  f  i  k  r  n  n  e
o  s  k  i  n  k  e  h  o  d  a  d  o
r  s  i  d  e  w  i  n  d  e  r  a  n
```

Outdoor Shape Hunt

Let's look for shapes again. But this time, head outside. Walk through your yard, your neighborhood, or a park. See if you can find each shape listed below. On the line, write where you found the shape.

- ❏ circle _____
- ❏ square _____
- ❏ triangle _____
- ❏ diamond _____
- ❏ oval _____
- ❏ straight line _____
- ❏ heart _____
- ❏ Z shape _____
- ❏ X shape _____
- ❏ W shape _____
- ❏ V shape _____
- ❏ U shape _____
- ❏ T shape _____
- ❏ S shape _____

What's Different?

Can you spot the 10 differences in these two pictures?

Timed Scavenger Hunt

Look at the list of materials. Can you find things made from each?

Set a timer for 10 minutes. See if you can gather the objects before the timer runs out. Be very careful with anything that is breakable. Afterward, write the name of each thing you found next to the word that tells what it is made from.

Find something that is made from . . .

❏ metal _____

❏ plastic _____

❏ rubber _____

❏ paper _____

❏ wood _____

❏ glass _____

❏ cloth _____

❏ cardboard _____

❏ stone _____

❏ leaves or flowers _____

What's Different?

Can you spot the 10 differences in these two pictures?

TECH *Timeout*

Geography Search

Find and circle the words in the puzzle.

state	lake	ocean	island
latitude	river	mountain	county
country	north	south	province
longitude			

```
l o n g i t u d e f i p
a c o u n t y i b h k r
t o r i v e r s d j m o
i u t s u v y l a k e v
t n h o o c e a n l n i
u t l u m o u n t a i n
d r j t s w z d c e g c
e y k h t x a s t a t e
```

A Gentle Giant

Solve the equations in each space below. Then, color the spaces using the color key to help you find the hidden picture.

14 = **blue**   15 = **green**   16 = **yellow**

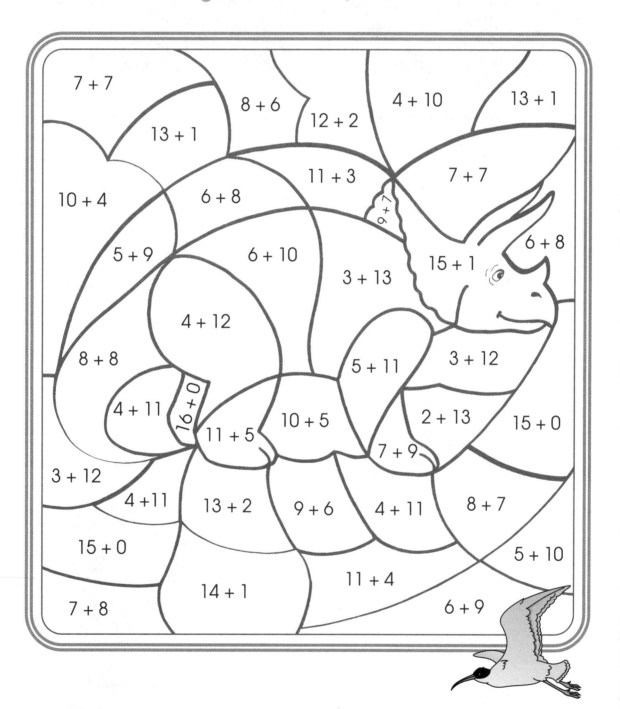

Find It   TECH*Timeout*   **Grade 2**

Book Hunt

This scavenger hunt is perfect for the next time you are at the library. Just be sure you are quiet and polite as you search. And don't forget to ask a librarian if you need help!

Try to find each book shown below. Write the titles on the lines.

Find . . .

❏ the book that is farthest from the check-out counter:

_____

❏ the biggest book in the children's section:

_____

❏ the smallest book in the children's section:

_____

❏ the nonfiction book with the highest
Dewey Decimal number:

_____

❏ the first book in the fiction section:

_____

❏ a book with pictures of ships and boats:

_____

❏ a book with a bird as a character:

_____

❏ a DVD with more than one copy to check out:

_____

❏ a book with a one-word title:

_____

❏ a book you have read:

_____

Musical Treasure Hunt

Find the 29 hidden items in the classroom next door.

- ❏ teacup
- ❏ flower pot
- ❏ sailboat
- ❏ pencil
- ❏ book
- ❏ lollipop
- ❏ screw
- ❏ lemon wedge
- ❏ pizza slice
- ❏ feather
- ❏ crayon
- ❏ hockey stick
- ❏ starfish
- ❏ music note
- ❏ butterfly
- ❏ leaf
- ❏ cherry
- ❏ popsicle
- ❏ paintbrush
- ❏ snake
- ❏ snowman
- ❏ umbrella
- ❏ donut
- ❏ mushroom
- ❏ candle
- ❏ golf club
- ❏ stocking
- ❏ flashlight
- ❏ baseball hat

Rocks and Minerals

Find and circle the words in the puzzle.

slate	obsidian	sand	topaz
agate	gem	stone	quartz
salt	lava	ruby	diamond
granite			turquoise

```
b  a  g  a  t  e  r  r  o  g  e  m
i  s  r  q  j  g  u  d  b  d  s  k
m  l  a  j  q  o  b  i  s  s  t  p
s  a  n  d  u  m  y  a  i  f  o  s
k  t  i  l  a  v  a  m  d  t  n  a
f  e  t  u  r  q  u  o  i  s  e  l
e  z  e  y  t  h  a  n  a  l  u  t
t  o  p  a  z  x  w  d  n  v  c  e
```

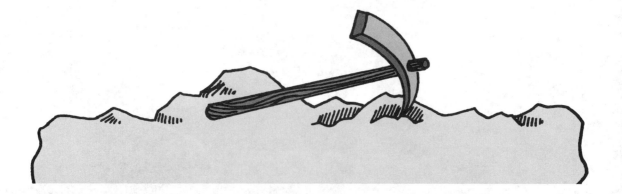

Outdoor Timed Scavenger Hunt

Review the list of words. Then, head outside to your backyard or a park.

Set a timer for 10 minutes. See if you can find items that fit the descriptions before the timer runs out. Afterward, write the name of each object next to the word that describes it.

Find something that is . . .

❏ tall _____

❏ thick _____

❏ yellow _____

❏ old _____

❏ sharp _____

❏ square _____

❏ wet _____

❏ tiny _____

❏ alive _____

❏ smooth _____

For an extra challenge, give this list to a friend or two. Have a race to see who can find all the items first.

What's Different?

Can you spot the 10 differences in these two pictures?

Measuring Scavenger Hunt

How do you measure up? Try this scavenger hunt to find out!

All you need is a ruler. If you have a yardstick or tape measure, those will work even better. Use the tools to find things that are described below. Write what you find on the lines.

Find something that is . . .

❏ less than 1 inch long.

_____

❏ exactly 1 foot long.

_____

❏ about 8 inches long.

_____

❏ about 2 feet long.

_____

❏ more than 3 feet long.

_____

❏ exactly 18 inches long.

_____

❏ exactly 5 inches long.

_____

❏ about 30 inches long.

_____

For some extra measuring practice, complete the sentences below.

The kitchen sink is about _____ inches wide.

My toothbrush is about _____ inches long.

The table is about _____ inches high.

The front door is about _____ inches wide.

Water Sports

Find and circle the words in the puzzle.

knife		spear	aqua-lung
skiing	mask	wet suit	ropes
paddle	diving	oxygen	float
polo	swimming		weights

```
r  o  p  e  s  d  p  a  d  d  l  e
w  e  p  u  p  k  s  q  t  x  s  c
e  r  o  w  e  t  s  u  i  t  k  i
i  f  l  o  a  t  m  a  s  k  i  o
g  f  o  l  r  p  v  l  j  n  i  q
h  d  i  v  i  n  g  u  w  i  n  m
t  h  o  x  y  g  e  n  n  f  g  g
s  w  i  m  m  i  n  g  b  e  z  a
```

Grocery Store Color Hunt

The grocery store is a colorful place. It is perfect for a color hunt! Bring this page with you the next time you go to the grocery store. Look for foods that match each color shown below. Write what you find next to its color.

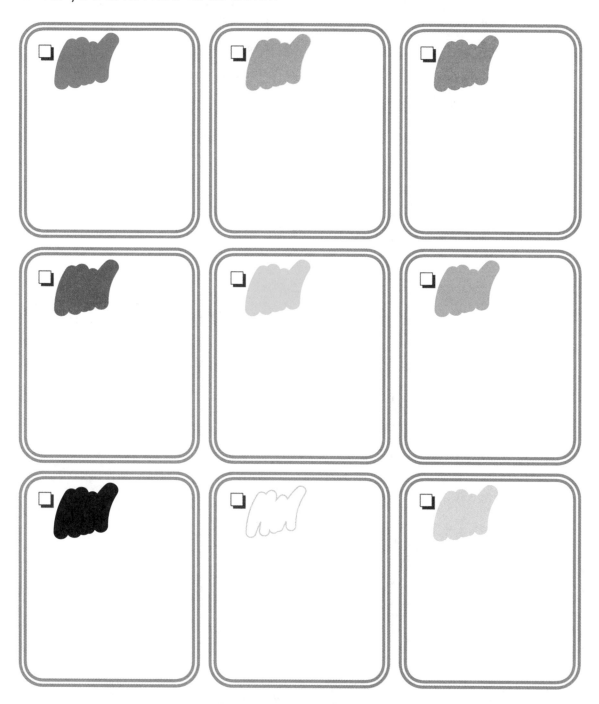

Name:

Texture Hunt

Peel the paper off of a dark crayon. Grab a few pieces of paper and head outside.

Lay the paper against tree trunks, sidewalks, and patio furniture. Look for anything else that has an interesting texture. Rub the crayon over the paper to copy the textures.

Cut out a square from each texture. Paste the squares in the grid below. Then, ask a friend to guess where each rubbing came from.

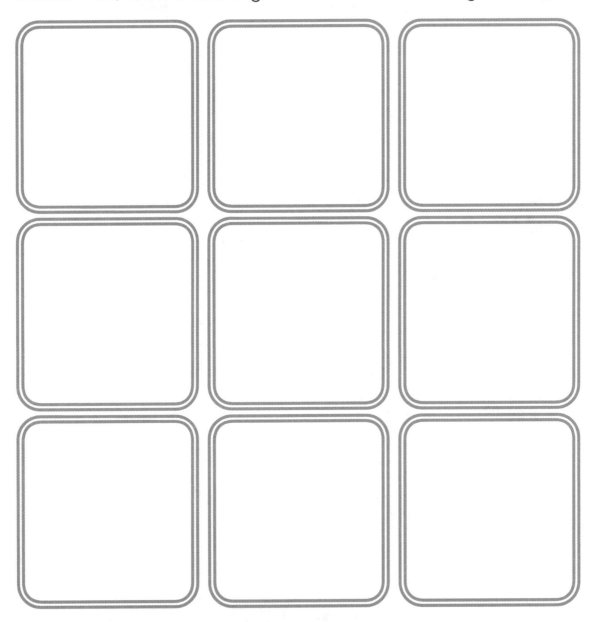

What's Different?

Can you spot the 10 differences in these two pictures?

Community Helpers

Find and circle the words in the puzzle.

firefighter	dentist	mechanic
doctor	teacher	baker
nurse	clerk	plumber
bus driver	judge	barber

```
w n u r s e p l u m b e r
d x a z y t e a c h e r j
o c b c f j a p b l k i d
c l d a g h u c m d h b e
t e w u k r q d o e i a n
o r z v t e s n g f g r t
r k b u s d r i v e r b i
u m e c h a n i c t s e s
f i r e f i g h t e r r t
```

Outdoor Alphabet Hunt

Get 26 index cards. Write each letter of the alphabet on an index card.

Then, head outside with the cards. Look for something that starts with **A**, such as an acorn. Write **acorn** on the back of the card.

Keep going until you find something for every letter. But look out—some letters are tricky!

A B C D E
F G H I J
K L M N
O P Q R S
T U V W
X Y Z

Dino Dig Treasure Hunt

Find the 25 hidden items in the scene next door.

- ❏ human tooth
- ❏ kite
- ❏ cane
- ❏ lemon slice
- ❏ piece of popcorn
- ❏ smiley face
- ❏ key
- ❏ mushroom
- ❏ bell
- ❏ light bulb
- ❏ bowl
- ❏ banana
- ❏ paintbrush
- ❏ pear
- ❏ leaf
- ❏ tepee
- ❏ cracked egg
- ❏ stocking
- ❏ button
- ❏ heart
- ❏ sailboat
- ❏ party hat
- ❏ soup can
- ❏ paperclip
- ❏ pizza slice

Machine Search

Find and circle the words in the puzzle.

car	typewriter	saw	motor
plane	jet	lathe	forklift
motorcycle	crane	tractor	computer
drill			punch

```
f  d  w  o  u  t  m  t  a  p  j  c
o  m  o  t  o  r  c  y  c  l  e  o
r  e  m  p  v  a  s  l  r  a  t  m
k  s  o  q  w  c  a  r  a  n  p  p
l  a  t  h  e  t  x  r  n  e  u  u
i  w  o  h  i  o  k  j  e  c  n  t
f  f  r  g  d  r  i  l  l  b  c  e
t  y  p  e  w  r  i  t  e  r  h  r
```

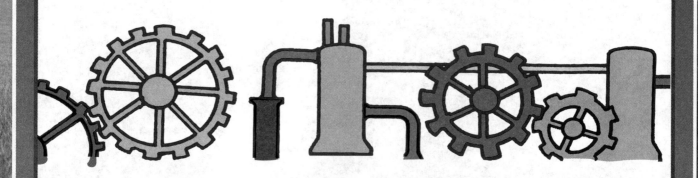

What's Different?

Can you spot the 12 differences in these two pictures?

Outdoor Scavenger Hunt

On a nice day, head out on a walk through your neighborhood or a park. Can you find everything shown below? Check off each thing as you find it.

☐ stick on the ground

☐ squirrel

☐ someone on a bike

☐ birds in a tree

☐ white stones

☐ flowers

☐ someone walking a dog

☐ pinecone

☐ a fence

Sports Search

Find and circle the words in the puzzle.

volleyball	swim	cross country
tennis	soccer	gymnastics
cheerleading	softball	dance

```
c h e e r l e a d i n g s
s g y m n a s t i c s d o
o m d i c y c e s j i b f
c j b a e f l n k w r c t
c a e d n h i n r a i z b
e z y t x c o i t x l m a
r v t r a i e s a r a f l
a v o l l e y b a l l s l
c r o s s c o u n t r y l
```

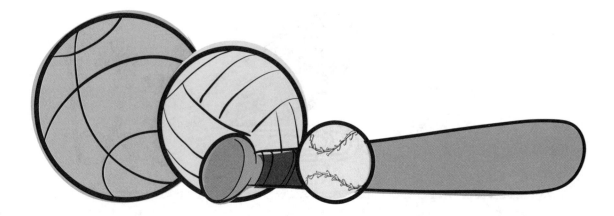

Knock Knock Scavenger Hunt

You will need an adult or older sibling to go with you on this scavenger hunt.

Start by making a list of five to 10 neighbors you know well. Then, grab a large bag and the list below. Go to each neighbor's house, and see which item they can give to you. Be polite, and explain that you are on a scavenger hunt. Do not gather more than two items from the same house.

❏ an old magazine

❏ a rubber band

❏ an empty cereal box

❏ a button

❏ a paperclip

❏ a catalog

❏ a paper towel

❏ a penny

❏ a red ink pen

❏ safety pin

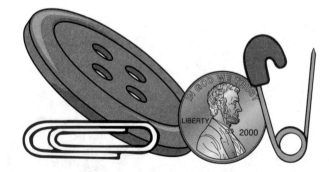

Name:

Fashion Frenzy

Find and circle the words in the puzzle.

sunglasses		
scarf	mittens	coat
sundress	shorts	boots

s	u	n	g	l	a	s	s	e	s
h	c	b	d	k	f	r	p	n	u
o	a	a	e	g	b	s	m	o	n
r	c	e	r	f	o	e	i	c	d
t	w	c	v	f	o	j	t	d	r
s	z	o	e	m	t	a	t	z	e
e	x	a	s	t	s	m	e	c	s
r	h	t	g	o	f	p	n	r	s
i	c	h	e	s	t	e	s	d	f

Scavenger Hunt

An Arctic tern has been migrating through the pages of this book. Can you find all the pages it has flown through?

List the 14 pages on the lines below.

Play It

Exercise It!

Grab a piece of sidewalk chalk and head outside. It's time to get moving!

Draw four big squares on the ground. Write the names of these exercises in the squares. Write one in each square.

Choose a square to start in. Count to 30 as you do the exercise for that square. Then, move quickly to a different square. Count to 30 as you do the next exercise. Keep going like this until you have visited all four squares.

Taking Aim

This simple game will test your throwing skills. All you need are four empty plastic bottles and some sheets of paper.

Line up the four bottles on a table or wall. Leave a few inches of space between each bottle. Then, use the sheets of paper to make paper balls. Start with about 10 balls.

Walk about 10 steps away from the bottles. Throw the paper balls at the bottles. See how many throws it takes to knock down all four bottles.

Set up the bottles in a line again. Gather up the paper balls. Try again, and see if you can do better the second time.

When you are done, save the bottles and paper balls to play again another time. If you do not want to save them, be sure to recycle everything.

Trail Blazing

A **blaze** is a colorful mark on a tree or a rock. It shows a hiker where the trail goes. **Trail blazing** is when you mark a new trail with blazes.

Go trail blazing in your yard, your neighborhood, or at a park. Cut a piece of colorful fabric into strips. As you take a walk, tie the strips to branches, signposts, or fences. Make sure you can see the last strip as you tie a new one.

Then, take a friend on a walk. Follow the same route to see if your friend can follow the blazes. Clean up the strips when you finish.

Sponge Throw

You may get wet playing this game, so choose a warm day for it.

You will need some sidewalk chalk, a few sponges, a bowl of water, and a pair of scissors to play. You will also need a sidewalk or driveway to play on.

Cut each sponge in half. Make a pile of sponges next to the bowl of water. (Cut up extra sponges if you're playing with a partner.) Dip a sponge in the water, and toss it as far as you can. Find the wet mark, and draw a line across the ground there. Write 50 on the far side of the line.

Now take two steps back toward the bowl of water. Draw another line. Write 40 in the space between the two lines. Take two more steps, draw a line, and mark the new space 30. Keep going until you have drawn five lines. You should have spaces marked 0, 10, 20, 30, 40, and 50.

Head back to the bowl and sponges. One at a time, throw a total of four sponges. You can use the chalk to keep track of the total number of points you score.

Take turns if you're playing with a partner. If you're playing alone, see if you can beat your own best score!

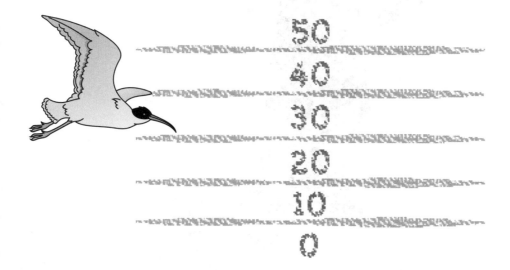

Exercise It!

Grab a jump rope and find some happy music. As soon as you turn on the music, start jumping rope. See how long you can jump as you listen to your favorite songs.

When you need to, take a break. Rest in between songs.

If jumping rope is too difficult, you can lay the rope on the ground. Jump back and forth over the rope as the music plays.

How many songs played before you needed a rest?

Shadow Animals

Have you ever pretended to be an animal? What kind of animal was it? In this activity, you can turn your shadow into an animal. You will need the help of a friend or family member.

● **What You Need**

- ❏ sidewalk chalk
- ❏ a driveway or sidewalk

● **What You Do**

1. On a sunny day, head outside to a place where you can clearly see your shadow. This activity works best earlier or later in the day, when your shadow is bigger.

2. Look at your shadow on the ground. Think of an animal you would like to be. Try to pose so your shadow looks a little bit like the animal. You can use your hands and arms to make extra legs, antlers, horns, or fins. Twist, crouch, or stretch your body to change your shadow's shape.

3. Have a friend use chalk to trace the outline of your shadow. Then, have your friend pose, and you can trace his or her shadow's outline.

4. Use the chalk to add details to your shadow animal. You can add fur, scales, or any other features. If the shadow shape is strange, you can make a shadow monster or a made-up animal. Let your imagination be your guide!

The Hunt Is On

- **What You Need**

  - ❏ ice cube trays
  - ❏ washable paints

- **What You Do**

  1. Fill two ice cube trays with water.
  2. Mix a few drops of paint into each section. Try to use a lot of different colors.
  3. Put the ice cube trays in the freezer. Wait several hours.
  4. Empty the colorful ice cubes into a bucket or large bowl. Ask a friend or family member to hide the ice cubes in different places outside.
  5. Now it's time for the hunt. Use the bucket or bowl to search for and gather the ice cubes. But hurry! If the day is too warm, they may not last long.

After you have found all the ice cubes, you can use them to paint. Just rub the ice cubes on a piece of watercolor paper!

Nature Stack

It is hard to build a tower in nature. But with some patience and practice, you can do it!

Start by gathering sticks, rocks, pieces of bark, pinecones, and other objects from outside.

Then, try to use them to build a tower.

Your tower does not need to be tall and skinny. Think about how the pieces can be put together so they do not fall. Your tower may look more like a pyramid. It may look more like a building. It may even look like a piece of modern art!

Keep trying until you find a way to stack all of your objects together.

Exercise It!

Grab a deck of cards, and get ready to move your body!

Choose three of the exercises below.

- ❏ sit-ups

- ❏ running in place

- ❏ jumping jacks

- ❏ push-ups

- ❏ touching toes

Shuffle the cards. Then, draw three cards from the deck. Use the numbers on the cards to tell you how many times you need to do each exercise. Face cards are worth 10. If you are running in place, run until you count the number on the card.

Did you get enough of a workout? If not, draw three more cards, and go again!

Weather Dancing

Some American Indian tribes perform rain dances. Invent your own weather dance!

Think of a type of weather you want it to be. Then, make your dance moves match the weather you want. Have an adult help you pick a song that mentions the kind of weather you are dancing for.

After you have practiced your dance a few times, perform it for your family!

Up and Down the Hill

Find a small hill outside. You may have one in your yard. You may need to head to a park or playground.

Go to the top of the hill. Now think about going back down. How many ways can you get down the hill?

Try each of the following:

- ❏ rolling
- ❏ running
- ❏ hopping
- ❏ skipping
- ❏ walking
- ❏ going backwards

Can you think of others?

When you cannot think of another way to get down the hill, try using each way to get back up the hill!

What Animal Are You?

This game is best with a lot of people, but even two can play.

One person starts the game by choosing an animal and acting like it. For example, if the player picked a cat, he might meow, lick his paw, and purr. The next players ask, "What animal are you?"

Here is where the game gets tricky. The player acting like a cat does not answer, "A cat." He answers by naming a different animal, and the next player must now act like that animal.

When a player answers by naming the animal they are acting like, they are out of the game. Keep going until only one player is left. He or she is the winner.

Exercise It!

This exercise is called "5 in 25." As you count down from 25, you will do five different exercises.

Run in place as you count: 25, 24, 23, 22, 21 . . .

Do five jumping jacks as you count: 20, 19, 18, 17, 16 . . .

Touch your toes five times as you count: 15, 14, 13, 12, 11 . . .

Lunge forward five times as you count: 10, 9, 8, 7, 6 . . .

Do five sit-ups as you count: 5, 4, 3, 2, 1.

25 . . .

20 . . .

15 . . .

10 . . .

5 . . .

0!

Target Practice

Do you know how to shoot a rubber band? This activity will help you improve your aim.

Find a large, flat piece of cardboard. With an adult's help, cut three circles out of the cardboard. Make one circle 12 inches wide, one 9 inches wide, and one 6 inches wide. Using a marker, label the biggest circle **1**, the medium circle **2**, and the smallest circle **3**.

Use painter's tape to hang the piece of cardboard in a doorway.

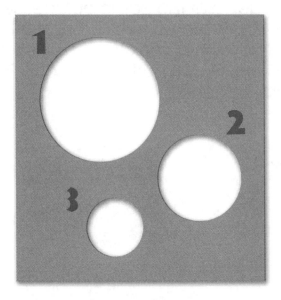

Now grab a handful of rubber bands. Walk about 10 steps away from the doorway. Take aim, and fire! Score 1, 2, or 3 points each time you shoot through a hole. Keep track of your total score. How many shots does it take you to reach 10 points?

Balloon Ball

How long can you keep a balloon in the air? Blow up a balloon and find out.

First, make a paddle by securely taping a large craft stick to a paper plate. Blow up a balloon and practice bouncing it in the air with your paddle.

If you make a second paddle, you can play with a partner. Bounce the balloon back and forth to each other. See how long you can keep the balloon from touching the ground.

For an extra challenge, take the game outside. Be sure to pick a day that is not too windy. Even a small breeze will make the game harder. You'll have to be quick on your feet! And if the balloon hits the ground, watch out! It might pop! You may need a few extra balloons on hand.

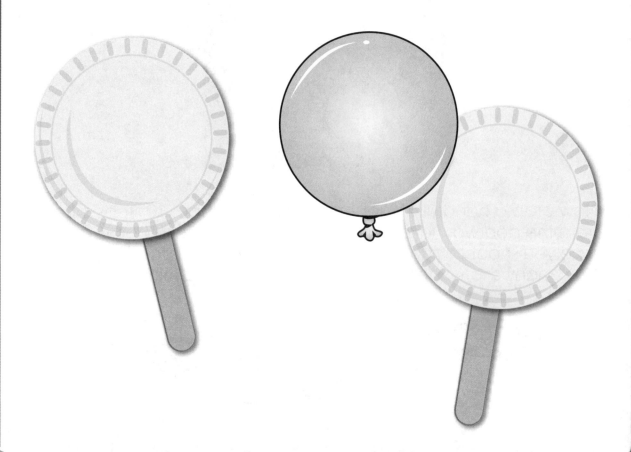

Zookeeping

Have you ever wanted to work at the zoo? Now is your chance!

Gather all of the toy animals you have. They can be stuffed animals, plastic animals, or even drawings of animals. Try to get a wide variety of different animals.

Pick one room in your house that will be the zoo. Think about where each animal or group of animals will live. At a real zoo, the animals are often arranged by type or where they live in the world. For example, reptiles are in one area, big cats in another, and fish someplace else. Arrange your animals in similar way.

Build living areas for each animal. You can use pillows, blocks, books, and furniture.

When you have finished building your zoo, it is time for a tour! Invite your friends or family to visit. Explain how you arranged the animals and why. Tell what you know about each kind of animal.

Silent Animal Charades

Sometimes it's okay to act like an animal, especially in this game.

You will need two or more people to play. Start by making a list of 20 animals. Write the name of each animal on an index card.

Shuffle the cards and place them facedown. The first player draws the card from the top of the deck. Without showing anyone the card, she acts like the animal written on it. But here is the tricky part: She cannot make any sounds.

The other players guess which animal she is being. The first player to guess correctly scores a point. If no one guesses, there are no points scored. Then, it is the next player's turn to draw a card.

Keep playing until all 20 cards have been used. The player with the most points wins.

Exercise It!

Time to get your blood pumping!

❏ Hop on one foot for 20 seconds.

❏ Swing your arms in circles for 20 seconds.

❏ Do jumping jacks for 20 seconds.

❏ Breathe deeply for 20 seconds.

Now do it all again!

Memory Game

How good is your memory? You can test it with this simple game.

Head outside and gather 20 small objects. Try to find a lot of different shapes, colors, and sizes. Some examples of what you might look for are rocks, acorns, pinecones, bark, sticks, and so on.

Set all of the items on a table in random order. Don't put them in neat rows. Don't spread them out too far or crowd them together.

Look carefully at all the items. Then, close your eyes or walk away from the table. Ask a friend or family member to remove one item without telling you what it is.

When you look again, can you tell which item is missing?

Puzzle Time

Do you like solving puzzles? In this activity, you will make your own jigsaw puzzle.

Ask permission to cut out a few magazine pages with pictures that you like. Glue the pages to pieces of poster board or thin cardboard, like a cereal box. Let the glue dry.

Next, cut each page into about 20 pieces. Mix all of the pieces together. Try to put them back together like a puzzle.

Backward Obstacle Course

Set up a safe, mini-obstacle course in a grassy area. You can set it up in a backyard or a park.

Use soft objects, like piles of cut grass or piles of leaves. You can use balls, hula hoops, and small toys. Arrange the items in a line. Decide which things you must jump or go around.

When it is time to race, you must go backward! Run or walk quickly backward through the course. Jumping backward will be a real challenge!

Ask a friend or family member to time you. Try again, and see if you can get through the course faster a second time.

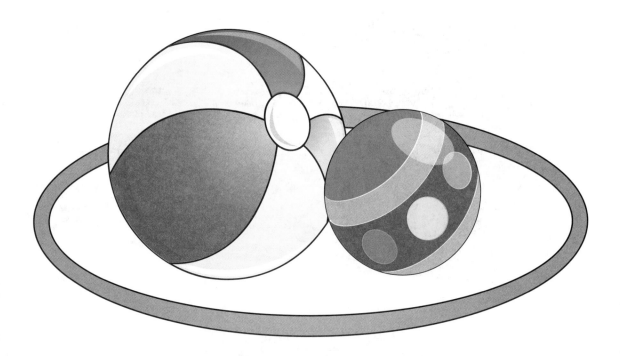

Stack 'Em Up

For this activity, you will need plastic drinking cups—lots of them. You will test your stacking skills.

Look at the pictures below. Can you stack the cups to make each shape?

Now try to stack as many cups as you can. Can you make a structure taller than you?

You can use the cups to make walls for a fort. But be careful—don't bump into them!

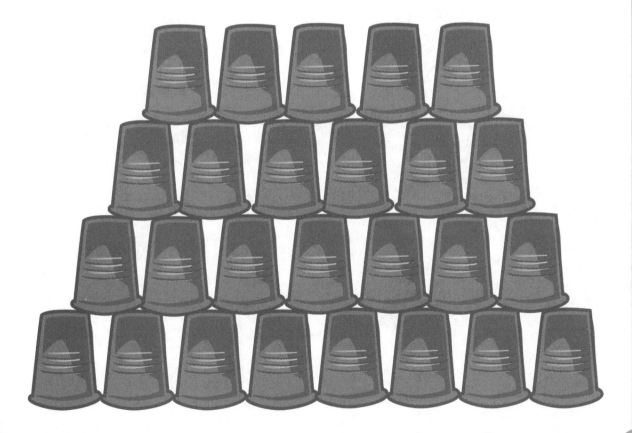

Exercise It!

Head outside to your yard or the sidewalk. You are going to get moving!

You will move in different ways for counts of 30. You can do the movements in any order you want. Be sure to move each way for the full count of 30.

Here is one way to do it:

You can run for 30 seconds, jump for 30 seconds, walk for 30 seconds, and then skip for 30 seconds.

That's only a 2-minute workout. You should be able to do it all a second time—or even a third!

Balloon Rocket

Get ready to blast off! You will build your own indoor rocket that will shoot across the room.

● **What You Need**

- ❏ a balloon
- ❏ paper clip, binder clip, or clothespin
- ❏ a straw
- ❏ tape
- ❏ a very long piece of string (long enough to stretch across a room or down a hallway)

● **What You Do**

1. Blow up the balloon. Then, use a clip or clothespin to pinch the opening closed. Do not tie the balloon closed.

2. Tape the straw onto the side of the balloon. Be sure the straw is pointing toward the open end of the balloon.

3. Put the string through the straw.

4. Attach one end of the string to something solid, like a door handle. Stretch the string as far as possible. Attach the other end to something solid as well.

5. Slide the balloon along the string to one end. Then, remove the clip or clothespin. As air shoots out of the balloon, it will zoom along the string!

Mini Bowling

Set up your own mini bowling alley. This game is perfect for a rainy day.

You will need painter's tape, a large marble or small rubber ball, and 10 pencil erasers. The erasers you need are the kind that fit on the end of a pencil.

Find a floor in your home that is smooth and does not have carpet. Use the tape to make your bowling lane. It should be about 12 inches wide and 4 feet long. Arrange the erasers on one end in a triangle. Kneel at the other end of the lane. Roll the marble or ball down the lane, and try to knock down the erasers.

 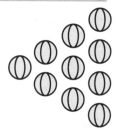

See how many rolls it takes to knock down all the erasers. If you play against a friend, you can keep score. Each person gets two tries to knock down the erasers. Score a point for each eraser that is knocked down.

Chalk People Fashion Show

On a nice day, head outside with some chalk and some crazy fashion ideas.

Lie down on the sidewalk or driveway. Have a friend use chalk to trace the outline of your entire body. Then, use chalk to add a face and hair. Now comes the fashion part.

Gather a crazy collection of clothing. You can use dress-up clothes or your real clothes. Be sure you have permission to bring the clothes outside.

Lay the clothing onto your chalk person. Think up silly ways to wear the clothes. Try out wild combinations of patterns and colors. If you have a camera, take some pictures.

Exercise It!

It's time to flex!

Pretend to be a jellyfish with long tentacles. Move slowly around the room. Imagine that you are gliding through the ocean. Stretch your arms from your shoulders to your wrists.

Flex each finger. Move your legs smoothly from your hips to your toes. Move your belly, back, and chest from left to right and front to back. Think about how you are moving. You should be slowly stretching several body parts at once.

If you want, add soft music or some ocean sounds as you glide and stretch.

Jam Session

Do you have a favorite song? It's time to crank it up and play along!

Find something simple that you can use to play along. Wooden spoons banging on metal pots or plastic bowls make great drums. Pick up a paper towel tube and sing through it. What other things can you find around the house for making music?

Turn up the music and jam along with a favorite song. Try to keep a steady beat.

You can try different kinds of music. Play along with a soft, slow song. Then, play along with a fast, loud tune.

Dirt Cake

Bakeries are filled with beautiful treats. But the cakes are usually the highlight. They are covered in colorful designs, pictures, flowers, or leaves—all made of icing. Have you ever wanted to design your own cake? You're hired!

Ask a grown-up for a pan or other kind of wide, deep dish. Be sure you are allowed to take it outside.

Fill the pan or dish with dirt. That is your cake! Now it is time to decorate.

Gather pretty things from nature, like stones, leaves, flowers, or acorns. Then, use them to create a design or picture on the "cake."

Invite some friend to make cakes of their own. Then, display all the cakes on a table or the ground. Tell your favorite part of each cake's decoration.

River Race

In this activity, you will make a river. All you need is a roll of aluminum foil and some water.

Find an area outdoors with a bit of a slope. A low hill or driveway will work well. Unroll a very long piece of foil. The piece can be 10 feet or longer if you want.

Carefully bend up the sides of the foil. You want to scrunch the foil sides so they are sturdy and hold their shape. The foil should look somewhat like a gutter. If you want, you can bend the long piece of foil so it turns different directions. You can also add more foil to make your "river" longer.

Once you have your "river" made, it's time to add water. If you have a hose outside, put it at the top end of the foil. Turn the water on just enough to make a small stream. It should flow down the foil and out the end.

If you don't have a hose, you can fill several large containers with water. You will need to pour the water slowly into your "river" by hand.

Now it is time for the river race. Find small objects to float down the river. You can use leaves or small pieces of cardboard. Experiment with different things to see which work best.

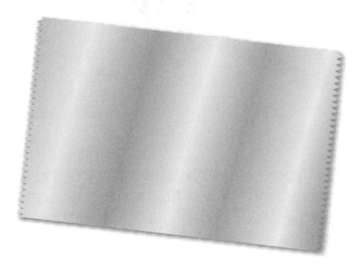

Catapult

After you make this catapult, you can use it for many different target games.

You will need eight craft sticks, a bottle cap, and some rubber bands.

Stack six craft sticks together. Wrap a rubber band tightly around each end of the stack to hold them together.

Next, stack two craft sticks together. Wrap a rubber band tightly around one end to hold them together.

Slide the big stack of craft sticks in between the other two craft sticks. Use another rubber band to hold the big stack in place between the two craft sticks.

Glue the bottle cap onto the end of the top stick.

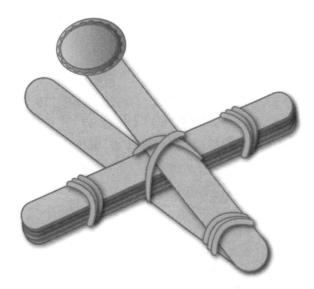

Now you can test your aim. Make small paper balls for your catapult. Try to fling them into a trashcan. You can also draw a target on a large piece of paper. Try to land the paper balls onto the target.

Exercise It!

How far will 100 steps take you? How about 200 steps?

Let's find out!

Choose a place to start. It can be inside your house. It can be outside in your yard or at a park.

Think about how far you will go after taking 200 steps. If you are inside, think about how many rooms your will walk through. If you are outside, look into the distance. Think about where you will end up. Make a prediction.

Now start walking. Count each step you take. Stop when you reach 100. How far did 100 steps take you? Think again about how 200 steps will take you. Make a new prediction.

Start walking again. Stop when you reach 100 again. Now you've gone 200 steps. Was your prediction correct?

Icy Swim

For this activity, you will need plastic eggs, ice cubes, a wading pool, and a warm day.

Start by filling the wading pool with water. Then, put an ice cube in each of the plastic eggs. Divide the eggs by color. Have friends help you hide the eggs outside. Each person will hide eggs of only one color.

Now it's time for an egg hunt! Have each friend search for eggs they did not hide. As your friends find the eggs, they should dump the ice into the wading pool. The last friend to dump ice into the pool is the first one to jump in! Brrr!

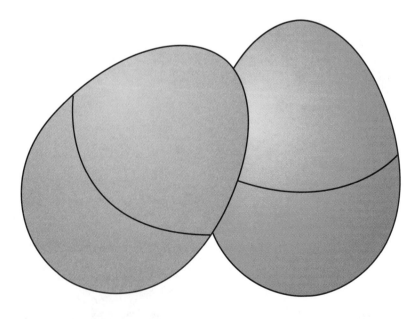

Silly Walk Parade

It's time to test your silly ability. What is your silliest way to walk?

Do you hop, trip, or jump? Walk backwards like a crab? Take a huge step and then tiny, little steps?

Practice different silly walks. Then, choose your silliest one.

Next, it's time for a silly walk parade. You can show off your silly walk alone. Or even better, you can invite friends to do their silliest walks too.

If you have a group of silly walkers, you can vote on who is the silliest. The only rule is that you cannot vote for yourself.

Ring Toss

You can make your own ring toss game with some paper plates and a paper towel roll.

First, glue the empty paper towel roll onto a paper plate so it is standing straight up.

Next, cut out the inside part of several paper plates. Leave about 2 inches around the outside. These are the rings you will toss.

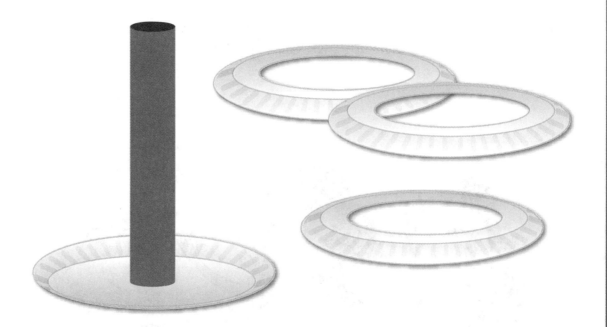

Let the game begin! Toss the rings onto the paper towel roll. Score a point each time you ring the paper towel roll.

If you find the game too easy, move farther away. If the game is too hard, move a bit closer.

Exercise It!

These 50 movements will really get your blood pumping. Be sure to do them quickly! And count out loud to 5 as you do each one.

- ❑ Stand on your tiptoes five times.

- ❑ Kick your legs five times.

- ❑ Bend your knees five times.

- ❑ Jump five times.

- ❑ Touch your toes five times.

- ❑ Twist back and forth at your waist five times.

- ❑ Punch the air five times.

- ❑ Clap your hands above your head five times.

- ❑ Shrug your shoulders five times.

- ❑ Tilt your head side to side five times.

Rollin' Rollin' Rollin'

This dice game is fast and fun. The goal is try to roll all of the same number.

Gather all the dice you can find. Using 10 dice is best, but you can use as many as you want.

Set a timer for one minute. Then, start rolling! Roll all the dice at once. Look for the number that comes up the most. Set those dice aside. Whatever number they show, that is the number you are trying roll.

Now grab the rest of the dice and roll them again. Each time you roll, set aside the dice that match the number from the first roll. Keep rolling until you have all the dice showing the same number. Could you do it before the timer ran out?

Try other ways to play this game. Use six dice, and try to roll the numbers 1 through 6. Or you can choose a number to roll before you begin. If you have plenty of dice, you can play against a friend. See who can roll all the same number first.

Chalk Town

Welcome to Chalk Town! The best thing about it is that you are in charge. You get to design the roads, buildings, and parks. There is one odd thing about Chalk Town. None of the roads are straight! They curve, swerve, twist, and spiral.

Head outside with some sidewalk chalk. It is time to draw your own Chalk Town. Remember the rule: no straight roads. Make the roads twisty and curvy. They can be as wild as you want them to be.

When you are done drawing roads, add some buildings. Think about what a town needs to have. Where will the school be? What about a hospital? Where do you live? Place the buildings wherever you want them to be. Then, think about parks, pools, forests, and other outdoor spaces. Add those next.

When your Chalk Town is finished, grab some toy cars. Drive them around the town. Pretend you are a tour guide. Show off the interesting and important places in Chalk Town.

Disc Golf

Set up a disc golf course in your yard or at a park. You will need a flying disc, of course. You will also need some targets to use for each "hole" on the course. The targets can be buckets, hula hoops, or other toys. Spread the targets around the area where you will be playing.

You can also make little flags with paper and sticks. Make enough flags to equal the number of targets. Then, write numbers on the flags for each hole. Stick the flags in the ground to show where you will start throwing for each hole.

Keep track of how many throws it takes to hit each target. When you have played each hole, add up your total number of throws. The lowest number is the winner.

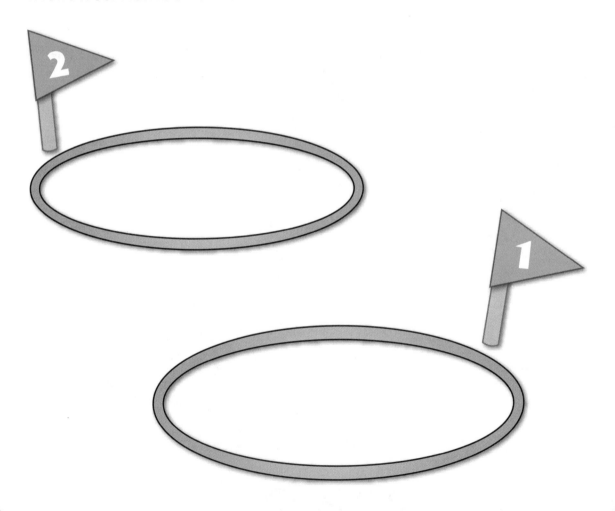

Exercise It!

Running is a simple way to get your blood pumping. It builds muscles and burns energy.

Find something outside that you can run around. It can be your house, your yard, a playground, or a sports field.

Now roll a die. Whatever number you get, that's how many times you need to run around it! If you roll a low number, try to run really fast. If you roll a high number, you might want to run a little more slowly.

Ice Cream Shop

What is your favorite flavor of ice cream? If you like more than one flavor, you can sell them in your ice cream shop!

This pretend game is simple to set up. All you need is colored paper, scissors, tape, and some large plastic containers. A big spoon for scooping is good to have, too.

Start by making some ice cream cones. Use brown paper. First, cut the paper into the shape below. Then, you can roll the paper into the shape of a cone. Use a couple of pieces of tape or staples to hold the cone shape. Make plenty of cones for your customers!

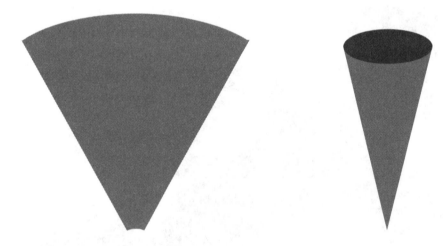

Next, use colored paper to make scoops of ice cream. This part is simple. Just crumple the colored paper into balls. Put the different colors into separate containers.

Now you want to label the containers. For each color, think of a flavor. You can have normal flavors, like chocolate, strawberry, mint, and vanilla. Or you can have silly flavors, like mud, ladybug, grasshopper, and chalk!

Set up your ice cream shop, and invite friends to "buy" some treats. Use the big spoons to pick up the scoops and set them in the cone.

Categories Game

Put your thinking cap on for this game.

Start by writing the letters of the alphabet down the left side of a piece of paper.

Next, choose a category. You can come up with your own idea, or you can choose one of the categories listed below.

- ❏ animals
- ❏ places
- ❏ boys' or girls' names
- ❏ sports or games
- ❏ foods
- ❏ famous people

Now, write something for each letter of the alphabet that fits the category. Some letters will be harder than others.

For an extra challenge, set a timer. How many letters can you complete in 10 minutes? 5 minutes? 1 minute?

A B C D E F G H I J
K L M N O P Q R S
T U V W X Y Z

Memory Card Game

How good is your memory? Test it with this simple card matching game.

Start with a normal deck of cards. Remove all the face cards (the kings, queens, and jacks). You will be left with 40 cards.

Shuffle the cards (or have an adult help you shuffle). Then, deal out all the cards face down. Deal the cards so you have five rows with eight cards in each row.

Set a timer. Then, turn over one card. Choose a second card and turn it over. If the two cards show the same number, you can remove them. If they are not the same number, turn them both back over. But try to remember which cards they were. The goal is to turn over matching pairs so you can remove them. Keep turning over cards, two at a time, until you have removed all the cards.

How long did it take? Try the game again and see if you can do it faster the second time.

Exercise It!

It's time to dance like an animal! Put on some fun, upbeat music. Then, pretend to be each of these animals as you dance to the music. Dance like each animal for a minute or so, and then switch. Be wild, have fun, and get your body moving!

Dance like …

❏ a snake.

❏ a monkey.

❏ an octopus.

❏ a penguin.

❏ a lion.

Tiny Snowman

The next time it snows, see if you can make a tiny snowman. How small can you make him?

Roll up little snowballs and stack them. Use very small twigs for arms. You can put an acorn cap on his head for a hat. Small pebbles could work for eyes. Be patient. Working with such small parts can be tricky.

It might not take long to make such a small snowman. You can probably make a whole snow family!

When you are done, take a close-up photograph of your little people.

Even if you do not have snow, you can make little people. Just use clay or colored play dough!

Balloon Kite

The next time you have a helium balloon, try this activity. It works best on a calm day with no breeze. You will need to find a wide open space. There should be no trees or power lines nearby. A park or playing field is perfect.

Take off the string that is tied to balloon. Grab a spool of thin thread. Tie the end of the thread to the balloon. Now slowly let out the thread. The balloon will rise higher and higher as you let out more thread.

How high will the balloon go? At some point, the weight of the thread will be too heavy for the balloon. It will not go any higher.

If you have more than one balloon, you can tie them all to the same piece of thread. How high will the balloons go now?

Connections

This game will get you thinking about how everything is connected. Even two things that seem totally different probably have something in common.

Gather 10 items from your room or house. Do not think too hard about what you grab. The things should be random. For example, you might gather a paper clip, a toy car, a bottle cap, a chopstick, a coin, a stuffed animal, a leaf, a pen, a book, and a crayon.

Lay out the things you collected. Now think about connections. Choose two items and tell one way they are connected. You could choose the pen and the crayon. They are both things to write with. Set them both aside. Then, you could pick the paper clip and coin. They are both made of metal. Set those aside. Keep going until you have removed all the items.

Exercise It!

It's time to go swimming! Even if it is winter, don't worry. You aren't going to get wet.

Lie down on your belly. Lift your arms and legs off the floor. Pretend to swim!

Slowly count to 20 as you "swim."

Now roll over on your back. Slowly count to 20 as you "swim" the backstroke.

Next, invent your own swim stroke. Slowly count to 20 as you make the moves for your new way to "swim."

Suction Up

For this game, you will need a straw, mini marshmallows, and a container. You will also need strong lungs!

The container can be a bottle, bowl, or cup. A tall bottle makes a great challenge. Just be sure the mini marshmallows will fit into the bottle's opening.

Lay about a dozen marshmallows on the table. Then, put the straw in your mouth. Using suction, pick up the marshmallows one at a time. Drop them into the container.

Set a timer for 1 minute. See if you can get all 12 marshmallows into the container before time runs out.

You can also challenge a friend to a race. See who can complete the task first.

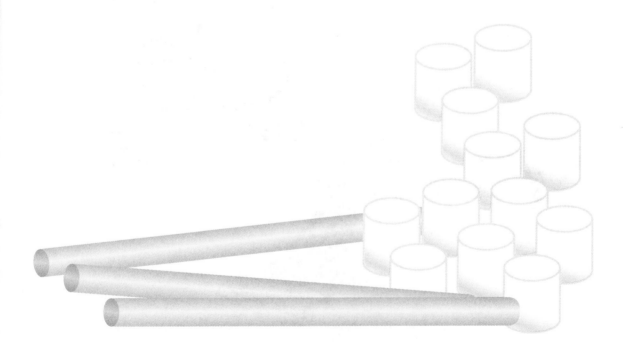

Hidden Message

Find the words from the word bank in the puzzle. Color them. Then, starting at the top and moving from left to write, find the letters that are left in the puzzle. Write the letters on the lines below. They will spell out a secret message. Do what the message tells you to do!

run   leaps   jump   run   wiggle   hop   squat   bounce   dance

D	O	T	J	H	B	E	C
R	A	B	U	W	O	A	R
L	K	A	M	C	U	R	U
O	H	O	P	S	N	S	N
S	Q	U	A	T	C	T	H
E	D	A	N	C	E	R	O
O	W	I	G	G	L	E	M
R	U	N	L	E	A	P	S

__ ___ ____ __ __

_____ ___ ____.

Answer Key

Crack the Code

Use the secret code to unlock the answer to a joke.

Why can't you play basketball with pigs?

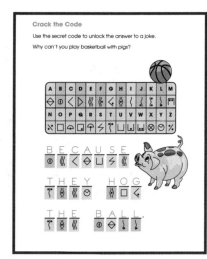

BECAUSE
THEY HOG
THE BALL.

68

Sudoku Challenge

Complete the sudoku puzzle. Every row and column must contain the numbers **5, 6, 7,** and **8.** Do not repeat the same number twice in any row or column.

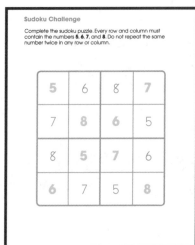

5	6	8	7
7	8	6	5
8	5	7	6
6	7	5	8

69

Crossword Opposites

Write the correct opposite into the crossword.

● **Across**
1. opposite of new
2. _____ is the opposite of loud.
5. opposite of up
6. If something is small, it is not _____.

● **Down**
1. _____ is the opposite of in.
3. opposite of over
4. If you are _____ then you are not near.

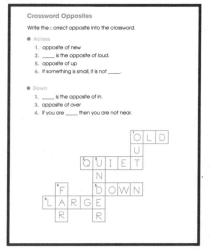

70

Journey to the Pyramids

Help the dog visit the Pyramids of Giza.

71

Secret Code

Decode the message using the symbols below.

C A T

F I S H I N G

72

What a Great Place!

Fill in the puzzle with words that name the pictures below. Use the word box to help you.

1. e r a s e r
2. t e a c h e r
3. c h a l k
4. c r a y o n s
5. b o o k
6. p e n c i l

The letters in the circles going down spell a mystery word. The word names a place where all these things can be found.

Write the mystery word.

_____ school _____

73

Going Places

Read the clues and use the words in the word box to complete the puzzle.

● **Across**
1. It is an automobile.
4. Hot air makes it rise into the sky.
6. This can carry heavy loads on the road.

● **Down**
2. This flies people from city to city.
3. This carries people and big loads on water.
4. It has two wheels and pedals.
5. This takes many people around the city.

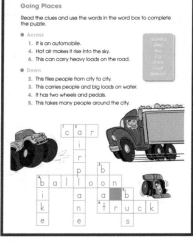

74

Answer Key

Winter Treat

Hop the marshmallows to the hot cocoa.

75

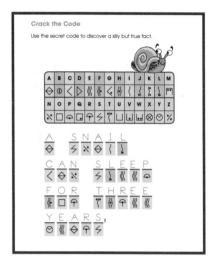

Crack the Code

Use the secret code to discover a silly but true fact.

A SNAIL
CAN SLEEP
FOR THREE
YEARS.

76

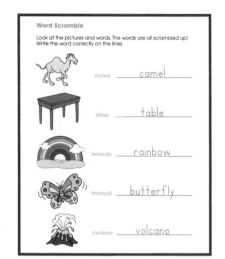

Word Scramble

Look at the pictures and words. The words are all scrambled up! Write the word correctly on the lines.

mcloa ___camel___

bltoe ___table___

wrinoab ___rainbow___

ttrebyult ___butterfly___

ovclona ___volcano___

77

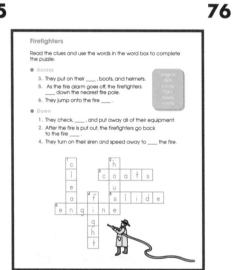

Firefighters

Read the clues and use the words in the word box to complete the puzzle.

● Across

  3. They put on their ___ , boots, and helmets.
  5. As the fire alarm goes off, the firefighters ___ down the nearest fire pole.
  6. They jump onto the fire ___ .

● Down

  1. They check, ___ , and put away all of their equipment.
  2. After the fire is put out, the firefighters go back to the fire ___ .
  4. They turn on their siren and speed away to ___ the fire.

78

Sudoku Challenge

Complete the sudoku puzzle. Every row and column must contain the numbers **1, 2, 3**, and **4**. Do not repeat the same number twice in any row or column.

1	2	4	3
3	4	2	1
4	1	3	2
2	3	1	4

79

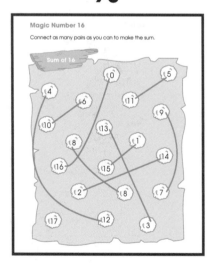

Magic Number 16

Connect as many pairs as you can to make the sum.

80

Crack the Code

Use the secret code to unlock the answer to a joke.

Why was the baby ant confused?

BECAUSE ALL
HIS UNCLES
WERE ANTS.

81

Answer Key

Loose Change

A little boy asks for your help. He put six coins in his pocket, and they all fell out! The coins add up to 95 cents. Can you help the boy find them?

Look at the coins below. Decide which coins were in the boy's pocket.

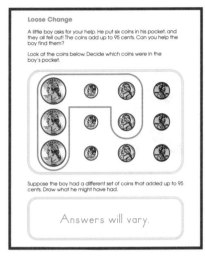

Suppose the boy had a different set of coins that added up to 95 cents. Draw what he might have had.

Answers will vary.

82

Sweet Spring

Read the clues and use the words in the word box to complete the puzzle.

● Across
2. It is the opposite of colder.
3. These bloom in the spring.
6. You can fly one outdoors in the spring.
7. Take your umbrella on days like this.

● Down
1. This is busy eating new leaves in spring.
4. It's fun to play here.
5. This is a good day to fly a kite.

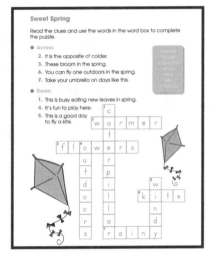

83

Play Ball!

Help the pup fetch her ball.

84

A Taste of Italy

Unscramble the letters to spell three different toppings on each pizza.

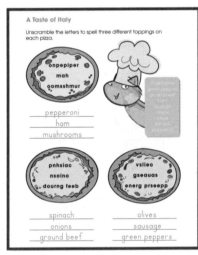

onpepiper — pepperoni
mah — ham
oomsshmur — mushrooms

pnhsiac — spinach
nsoino — onions
dourng feeb — ground beef

vslieo — olives
gseauas — sausage
energ prseepp — green peppers

85

Presto!

Exchange one letter from each pair of words to make two new words.

Example: lost — pace becomes post — lace.

Hint: The letter will not always be the first letter of each word.

hat — point _____ – _____

Answers will vary.

meat — nail _____ – _____

brain — get _____ – _____

like — bat _____ – _____

dear — way _____ – _____

86

Springtime Puzzler

Use the word lists to fill out the grid below.
Hint: Count the squares in the grid first to see where the words will fit.

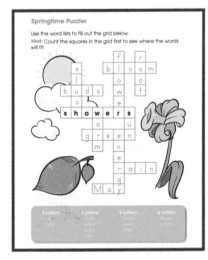

87

Hippopotamus Words

How many words can you make from the letters in HIPPOPOTAMUS?

MUST   TAP

Answers will vary

88

242

Answer Key

89

Snack Attack

Read the clues and use the words in the word box to complete the puzzle.

● **Across**
- 3. It comes from cows.
- 5. It can go in a pie.
- 7. It is good with jelly.

● **Down**
- 1. It is brown and sweet.
- 2. Rabbits like them.
- 4. It is made from milk.
- 6. It can be red, yellow, or green.
- 8. It is yellow and grows in a bunch.

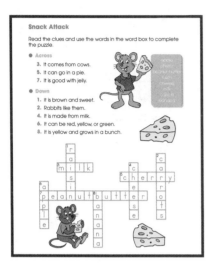

milk
cherry
peanutbutter

90

Unscramble Time

Unscramble each word. Be sure it goes with the meaning.

1. One who plays is called a
   lapeyr __p__ __l__ __a__ __y__ __e__ __r__

2. A round thing you can kick is a
   lalb __b__ __a__ __l__ __l__

3. A sweet treat to eat is
   danyc __c__ __a__ __n__ __d__ __y__

4. Something you can win is a
   pzire __p__ __r__ __i__ __z__ __e__

5. A person who wins is the
   nnewir __w__ __i__ __n__ __n__ __e__ __r__

6. One who sails a boat is a
   altsor __s__ __a__ __i__ __l__ __o__ __r__

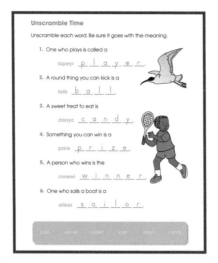

91

Race to the Finish Line

Help the racer reach the finish line.

92

Four Square

Starting with the top word in each square, change one letter at a time until the top word becomes the bottom word.

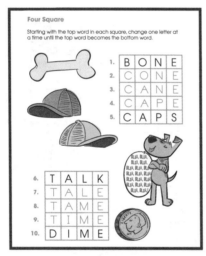

1. B O N E
2. C O N E
3. C A N E
4. C A P E
5. C A P S

6. T A L K
7. T A L E
8. T A M E
9. T I M E
10. D I M E

93

Animal Homes

Read the clues and use the words in the word box to complete the puzzle.

● **Across**
- 3. This is where bees make their honey.
- 4. This is a home for a clam.
- 6. Fish and frogs live here.
- 7. A bird makes this home.

● **Down**
- 1. Ants build one to live in.
- 2. This is where a spider lives.
- 5. A beaver builds a dam near this home.
- 8. A hole in this makes a good home for a squirrel.

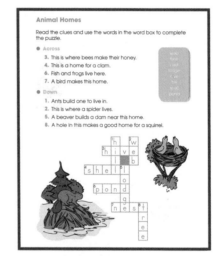

hive
shell
pond
nest

94

Time to Rhyme

Use the picture clues to match the rhyming words.

1. meat __f__ __e__ __e__ __t__
2. seal __w__ __h__ __e__ __e__ __l__
3. king __r__ __i__ __n__ __g__
4. mouse __h__ __o__ __u__ __s__ __e__
5. clock __s__ __o__ __c__ __k__
6. hair __b__ __e__ __a__ __r__
7. dog __f__ __r__ __o__ __g__
8. boat __g__ __o__ __a__ __t__

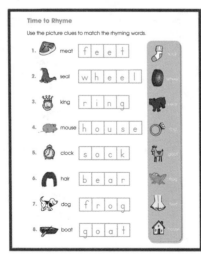

95

Compound Fun

Match each word in the word box with a word in the puzzle to make a new word.

1. s e a s h o r e
2. a i r p o r t
3. p a n c a k e
4. s u n s h i n e
5. d o o r k n o b
6. b a t h r o o m
7. f o o t b a l l
8. g o l d f i s h

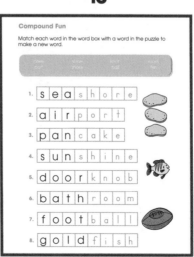

243

Answer Key

Word Scramble

Look at the pictures and words. The words are all scrambled up!
Write the word correctly on the lines.

linsa — snail

letrut — turtle

onstrme — monster

yonemk — monkey

ruqrtea — quarter

96

Sudoku Challenge

Complete the sudoku puzzle. Every row and column must
contain the numbers **1**, **2**, **3**, and **4**. Do not repeat the same
number twice in any row or column.

3	4	2	1
1	2	3	4
4	3	1	2
2	1	4	3

97

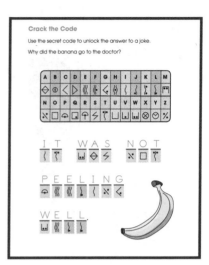

Crack the Code

Use the secret code to unlock the answer to a joke.

Why did the banana go to the doctor?

IT WAS NOT

PEELING

WELL.

98

Halloween Fun

Read the clues and use the words in the word box to complete
the puzzle.

● Across
2. Placed over your face
6. Carved pumpkin
7. Halloween month

● Down
1. Dracula is one of these.
3. Stirs potions in a cauldron
4. A house where ghosts
live is considered _____.
5. Disguise

2. mask
6. jackolantern
7. October

99

Head Hunter

Help the cat visit the Moai.

100

Secret Code

Write the letter for each symbol. Use the code
at the bottom of the page.

What happened when the Easter Bunny told a bunch
of silly jokes?

ALL OF
THE EGGS
CRACKED
UP

L A F O E T H G

S C K R D P U

101

Busy Year

Use the word lists to fill out the grid below.

Hint: Count the squares in the grid first to see where the words
will fit.

102

Answer Key

Sunshine Words

How many words can you make from the letters in SUNSHINE?

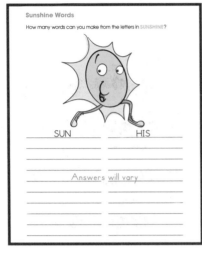

SUN   HIS

Answers will vary

103

Riddle Time

Use the word box on the next page to answer each clue in the squares on the right. Then, use your answers to fill in the letters of the riddle on the next page.

a. Not old
YOUNG
38 34 40 25 48

b. _____ and thank you
PLEASE
45 42 20 14 32 7

c. Police _____
STATION
41 9 24 4 46 11 15

d. Tells the time
WATCH
1 35 33 13 2

e. You smell with this
NOSE
19 17 26 22

f. Long stream of water
RIVER
21 12 31 37 36

g. Female nobility
QUEEN
5 6 31 44 47

104

h. What you do with a paddle
ROW
29 39 27

i. Japanese currency
YEN
30 28 12

j. You don't _____? (rhymes with "hay")
SAY
8 3 16

k. Second and last vowels in the alphabet, not including "y"
EU
43 18

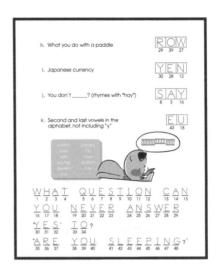

WHAT QUESTION CAN
1 2 3 4 5 6 7 8 9 10 11 12 13 14 15
YOU NEVER ANSWER
16 17 18 19 20 21 22 23 24 25 26 27 28 29
YES TO
30 31 32 33 34
"ARE YOU SLEEPING?"
35 36 37 38 39 40 41 42 43 44 45 46 47 48

105

Nursery Rhymes

Read the clues and use the words in the word box to complete the puzzle.

- **Across**
  2. Jack and Jill went up the _____.
  4. One, two, buckle my _____.
  7. Little Jack Horner sat in the _____.

- **Down**
  1. Hey diddle, diddle, the cat and the _____.
  3. Mary had a little _____.
  4. Little Bo-peep has lost her _____.
  5. Hickory, dickory, dock, the mouse ran up the _____.
  6. Little Boy Blue, come blow your _____.

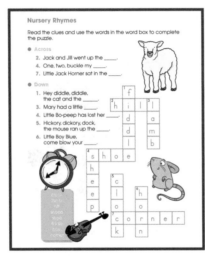

106

Trotting Right Along

Trot the pony to the giant carrot.

107

Spa Party!

Unscramble the words and write them on the lines.

nrmeacul   m a n i c u r e

varkmeoe   m a k e o v e r

delpurce   p e d i c u r e

filaca   f a c i a l

smasega   m a s s a g e

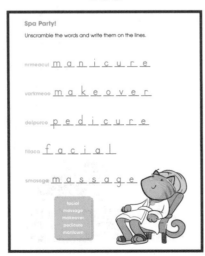

108

Award Shows

Write the missing letters **a, c, e, n,** or **o** for each word. Use the code at the bottom of the page.

O s c a r s

A c a d e m y

H o l l y w o o d

w i n n e r

r e d c a r p e t

A C E N O

109

245

At the Pool

Use the word lists to fill out the grid below.

Hint: Count the squares in the grid first to see where the words will fit.

t	o	w	e	l		R		A	P	S
A				O		A		i	
N				A		T		F		L	O	A	T
	W	H	I	S	T	L	E		L
D				O				g
I				N		S	u	n
D	I	V					a
R	E	S	T				r
			S	L	I	D	E

Facing the Sun

Read the clues and use the words in the word box to complete the puzzle.

● **Across**
1. A farm animal.
2. A buzzing bug.
4. A fruit.
6. A very tall plant.
7. The color of grass.
8. A big bird.

● **Down**
1. At night you _____.
3. A mouse eats _____.
5. You _____ food.
6. 2 + 1 = _____.
9. A part of a plant.

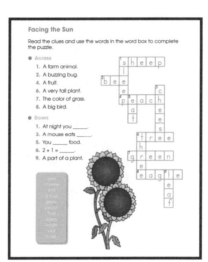

s h e e p
b e e
p e a c h
t r e e
g r e e n
e a g l e

Surprise Code!

Use the key to figure out the code and unscramble the answer to the question.

What has two heads, twenty-four legs and sharp, pointy teeth?

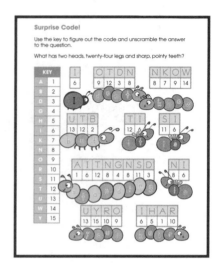

110   **111**   **112**

Shape Sudoku

Complete the sudoku puzzle. Every row and column must contain a ▲, ●, ♥, and ■. Do not repeat the same shape twice in any row or column.

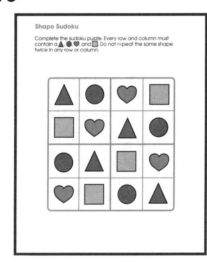

Slumber Party!

Write the missing letters **a, e, g, o, m,** or **s** for each word. Use the code at the bottom of the page.

p i l l o w f i g h t

g o s s i p

d a n c e

m o v i e s

m a k e o v e r s

A   E   G   O   M   S

113   **114**

To the Top of the Needle

Help the dog visit the Seattle Space Needle.

Start

Finish

Wild West

Use the word lists to fill out the grid below.

Hint: Count the squares in the grid first to see where the words will fit.

s p u r s
h a a c a c t u s
e n l a o h
e g h o s t t o w n e
p i p e o n b r
r e l e a i m
m a p e y f
r a i l f
r a w h i d e
e

115   **116**

117

Calendar Crossword

Read the clues and use the words in the word box to complete the puzzle.

● **Across**

2. It is a day for celebrating instead of working.
3. It can be measured in days, weeks, months, and years.
4. It can have 28 to 31 days.
6. You can hang it on a wall to keep track of the days.
8. This has twelve months.

● **Down**

1. This is the day you were born.
5. It has seven days.
7. A year has 365 of these.

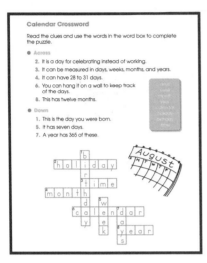

Across/Down answers: holiday, time, month, calendar, year, birthday, week, days

118

Pig Pen Puzzler

Use the word box on the next page to answer each clue in the squares on the right. Then, use your answers to fill in the letters of the riddle on the next page.

a. Makes you say, "Ouch!" P A I N 8 3 9 12

b. Class where you learn to add M A T H 25 14 7 5

c. Where bees live H I V E 17 14 19 41

d. Hospital room with a TV and magazines W A I T I N G 1 7 21 31 34 42 10

e. You bake in it O V E N 30 35 20 22

f. Piggy _____ B A N K 29 18 38 16

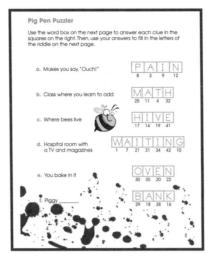

119

g. Swimming place P O O L 40 24 27 33

h. Opposite of "subtract" A D D 39 5 13

i. It lays eggs H E N 2 36 28

j. A penny is a _____ C O I N 23 6 37 15

k. Thirteenth letter of the alphabet M 26

WHAT DO A PIG AND INK HAVE IN COMMON?
BOTH LIVE IN A PEN.

120

World Traveler

Write the missing letters **a, d, e, n,** or **y** for each word. Use the code at the bottom of the page.

England
Germany
Finland
Japan
Italy

A D E N Y

121

A-Maze-ing Alien

Help the alien find his ride.

122

Found in Space

Read each riddle. Then, write the answer using one of the scrambled words from the word box.

1. This huge star lights the day. s u n
2. These shine at night. s t a r s
3. These are on the Moon. c r a t e r s
4. This is our home planet. E a r t h
5. This flies into space. s h u t t l e
6. This planet is red. M a r s
7. This planet has rings. S a t u r n
8. Astronauts do this in space. f l o a t

123

Slumbering Slippers

Read the clues and use the words in the word box to complete the puzzle.

● **Across**

4. Opposite of frown.
5. A small, slow-moving creature.
6. Opposite of rough.
9. Resting.
10. To slant or lean.
11. What your nose does.
13. Intelligent.
14. Ah …choo!

● **Down**

1. To shut with a bang.
2. A smooth, layered rock.
3. A cracking sound.
4. Very clever, like a fox.
6. To trip.
7. A kind of shoe.
8. Reptiles.
11. Frozen white flakes.
12. Something burning gives off.

Answers: smile, snail, smooth, sleeping, slope, smells, smart, sneeze

Answer Key

124

Who's at the Zoo?

Use the word lists to fill out the grid below.

Hint: Count the squares in the grid first to see where the words will fit.

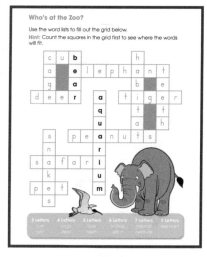

```
c  u  b        h
a     e  l  e  p  h  a  n  t
g     a              b     e
d  e  e  r     a     t  i  g  e  r
            q     t     t
            u     a     h
      s     p  e  a  n  u  t  s
      n     r
      s  a  f  a  r  i  u  m
      k           i
      p  e  t     u
      s           m
```

3 Letters	4 Letters	5 Letters	6 Letters	7 Letters	8 Letters
cub	deer	tiger	peanut	safari	elephant
pet				aquarium	

125

Castle Quest

Get the queen to her castle.

126

Sea Turtles Words

How many words can you make from the letters in SEA TURTLES?

EAR _____   RAT _____

Answers will vary

127

Holiday Crossword

Write the holidays from the word box in the puzzle. Then, find the secret word in the purple box.

```
1. C h r i s t m a s
2. F a t h e r 's  D a y
3. V a l e n t i n e 's  D a y
4. I n d e p e n d e n c e  D a y
5. A r b o r  D a y
6. E a s t e r
7. H a n u k k a h
8. V e t e r a n s  D a y
9. M o t h e r 's  D a y
```

The secret word is _____ celebrate _____

128

Land and Water

Read the clues and use the words in the word box to complete the puzzle.

● **Across**

2. This is a body of fresh water surrounded by land.
4. This is a very high hill.
6. This is low land between mountains or hills.

● **Down**

1. This is a very flat stretch of land.
3. This is a flowing stream of water.
5. This is a large body of salt water.

```
              p
              l  a  k  e
              a
r     m  o  u  n  t  a  i  n
i        c                n
v  a  l  l  e  y
e        a
r        n
```

129

Surf's Up!

Help the surfer catch some waves.

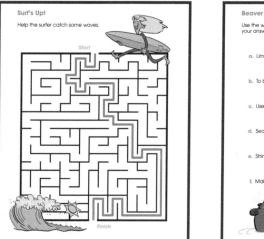

130

Beaver Clues

Use the word box to answer each clue in the squares. Then, use your answers to fill in the letters of the riddle on the next page.

a. Lima _____ — B E A N (11 35 32 43)

b. To be patient — W A I T (45 3 6 8)

c. Used to chew food — T E E T H (22 41 24 25 2)

d. Season — W I N T E R (1 39 37 4 12 26)

e. Stringed instrument — G U I T A R (42 51 29 20 13 16)

f. Makes bread rise — Y E A S T (19 28 18 17 30)

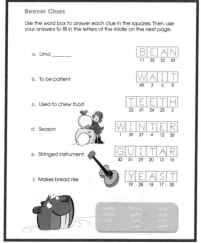

248

Answer Key

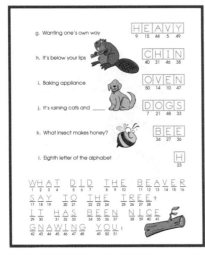

g. Wanting one's own way — H E A V Y (9 15 44 5 49)

h. It's below your lips — C H I N (40 31 46 38)

i. Baking appliance — O V E N (50 14 10 47)

j. It's raining cats and ___ — D O G S (7 21 48 33)

k. What insect makes honey? — B E E (34 27 36)

l. Eighth letter of the alphabet — H (23)

WHAT DID THE BEAVER SAY TO THE TREE? IT HAS BEEN NICE GNAWING YOU!

131

Kitten Family

How many words can you make from the letters in KITTEN FAMILY?

KITE   MAN

Answers will vary

132

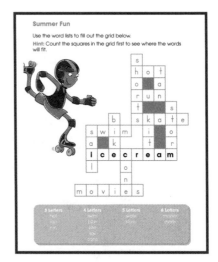

Summer Fun

Use the word lists to fill out the grid below.

Hint: Count the squares in the grid first to see where the words will fit.

133

Hidden Message

The answer to the question below is hidden on pages in this book. Look at each page number. Turn to that page, and find the red letter. Write the letter on the line.

This bird migrates from the Arctic to Antarctica and back again each year. It migrates farther than any other kind of bird—about 25,000 miles! Which bird is it?

A R C T I C (32 101 70 14 93 128)
T E R N (41 113 57 87)

134

The Wild West

Color the spaces with long vowel words brown. Color the spaces with short vowel words blue.

What did you color? boots

136

Indoor Shape Hunt

Shapes are everywhere. You just have to look carefully to see them. Take a walk through your house to hunt for shapes. See if you can find each shape listed below. On the line, write where you found the shape.

❏ circle   Answers will vary.
❏ square
❏ triangle
❏ diamond
❏ oval
❏ straight line
❏ heart
❏ Z shape
❏ X shape
❏ W shape
❏ V shape
❏ U shape
❏ T shape
❏ S shape

137

249

139

Nature Words

Find the nature words from the word box. Words can be across, down, diagonal, or backward.

140

What Is It?

Color the spaces with words that name vehicles yellow. Color the other spaces blue.

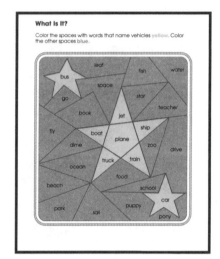

141

Kitchen Scavenger Hunt

Is it in the cupboard? Is it in the fridge? Maybe it is sitting right on the counter. Read the list of words below. For each word, find something in the kitchen that it describes. Write what you find on the line.

Answers will vary.

- sticky
- frozen
- sweet
- sharp
- shiny
- crunchy
- soft
- plastic
- metal
- wet
- fresh
- yellow
- tiny
- broken
- new
- striped

142

Tiny Dinos

Compsognathus was a tiny dinosaur that was no bigger than a chicken. Because it weighed about 5 pounds, Compsognathus was probably quick and light on its feet. It could chase down insects and other small animals, then use its sharp teeth and claws.

There are six of these tiny dinosaurs hiding in the picture below. Can you find them all? Circle each one.

143

Magic Number 11

Circle the pairs that equal 11.

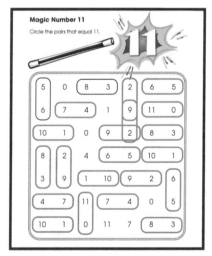

145

Nuts, Seeds, and Beans

Find and circle the words in the puzzle.

146

What's Different?

Can you spot the 10 differences in these two pictures?

147

Shirts and Shoes

If you put **s** and **h** together, they make the **sh** sound. How many things can you find in this picture that begin with **sh**? Circle them.

Write three more words that begin with **sh**.
Answers will vary.

149

Magazine Scavenger Hunt

Find a bunch of old magazines. Be sure no one wants them anymore. Then, grab a pair of scissors and look at the list below.

Flip through the pages. When you find something from the list, cut out the picture. Glue or tape the picture in the box or on another sheet of paper.

Find ...   Answers will vary.

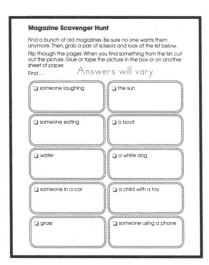

150

Shape Search

Find and circle the words in the puzzle.

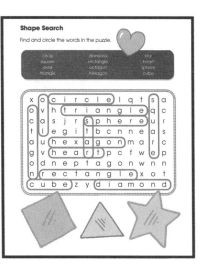

151

153

Answer Key

What's Different?

Can you spot the 10 differences in these two pictures?

154

Mystery Sentence

Color the following words in the puzzle green.

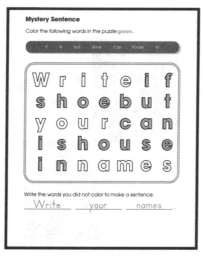

Write the words you did not color to make a sentence.

Write   your   names

155

Bicycle Words

Find and circle the words in the puzzle.

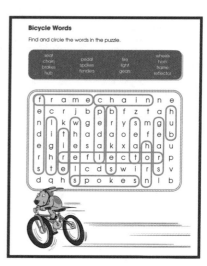

156

Match the Dinosaurs

Pachycephalosaurus had a thick bone on the top of its head. Knobs and spikes stuck out from this dome and the dinosaur's nose. Pachycephalosaurus may have crashed heads with rival dinosaurs to become the leader of the herd or to win mates.

Circle the two pictures below that are exactly alike.

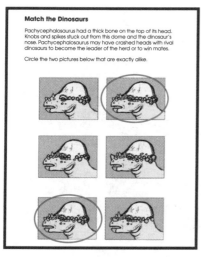

157

159

Reptile Search

Find and circle the words in the puzzle.

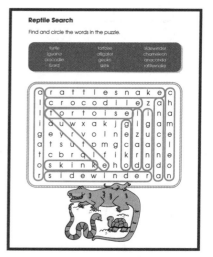

160

Outdoor Shape Hunt

Let's look for shapes again. But this time, head outside. Walk through your yard, your neighborhood, or a park. See if you can find each shape listed below. On the line, write where you found the shape.

- circle _____ Answers will vary.
- square _____
- triangle _____
- diamond _____
- oval _____
- straight line _____
- heart _____
- Z shape _____
- X shape _____
- W shape _____
- V shape _____
- U shape _____
- T shape _____
- S shape _____

161

What's Different?

Can you spot the 10 differences in these two pictures?

162

Timed Scavenger Hunt

Look at the list of materials. Can you find things made from each?

Set a timer for 10 minutes. See if you can gather the objects before the timer runs out. Be very careful with anything that is breakable. Afterward, write the name of each thing you found next to the word that tells what it is made from.

Find something that is made from . . .

- metal _____ Answers will vary.
- plastic _____
- rubber _____
- paper _____
- wood _____
- glass _____
- cloth _____
- cardboard _____
- stone _____
- leaves or flowers _____

163

What's Different?

Can you spot the 10 differences in these two pictures?

164

Geography Search

Find and circle the words in the puzzle.

state	lake	ocean	island
latitude	river	mountain	county
country	north	south	province
longitude			

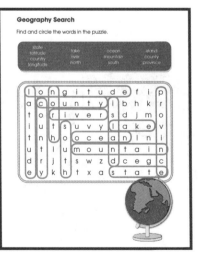

165

A Gentle Giant

Solve the equations in each space below. Then, color the spaces using the color key to help you find the hidden picture.

14 = blue   15 = green   16 = yellow

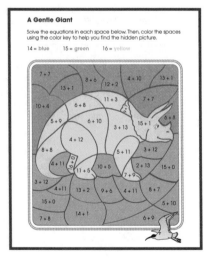

166

Book Hunt

This scavenger hunt is perfect for the next time you are at the library. Just be sure you are quiet and polite as you search. And don't forget to ask a librarian if you need help!

Try to find each book shown below. Write the titles on the lines. Find . . .

- ❑ the book that is farthest from the check-out counter:
  Answers will vary.
- ❑ the biggest book in the children's section:
- ❑ the smallest book in the children's section:
- ❑ the nonfiction book with the highest Dewey Decimal number:
- ❑ the first book in the fiction section:
- ❑ a book with pictures of ships and boats:
- ❑ a book with a bird as a character:
- ❑ a DVD with more than one copy to check out:
- ❑ a book with a one-word title:
- ❑ a book you have read:

167

169

Rocks and Minerals

Find and circle the words in the puzzle.

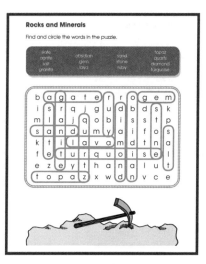

170

Outdoor Timed Scavenger Hunt

Review the list of words. Then, head outside to your backyard or a park.

Set a timer for 10 minutes. See if you can find items that fit the descriptions before the timer runs out. Afterward, write the name of each object next to the word that describes it.

Find something that is . . .

- ❑ tall — Answers will vary.
- ❑ thick
- ❑ yellow
- ❑ old
- ❑ sharp
- ❑ square
- ❑ wet
- ❑ tiny
- ❑ alive
- ❑ smooth

For an extra challenge, give this list to a friend or two. Have a race to see who can find all the items first.

171

What's Different?

Can you spot the 10 differences in these two pictures?

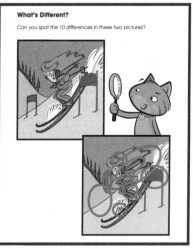

172

Measuring Scavenger Hunt

How do you measure up? Try this scavenger hunt to find out!

All you need is a ruler. If you have a yardstick or tape measure, those will work even better. Use the tools to find things that are described below. Write what you find on the lines.

Find something that is . . .

- ❑ less than 1 inch long.
  Answers will vary.
- ❑ exactly 1 foot long.
- ❑ about 8 inches long.
- ❑ about 2 feet long.
- ❑ more than 3 feet long.
- ❑ exactly 18 inches long.
- ❑ exactly 5 inches long.
- ❑ about 30 inches long.

For some extra measuring practice, complete the sentences below.

The kitchen sink is about _____ inches wide.
My toothbrush is about _____ inches long.
The table is about _____ inches high.
The front door is about _____ inches wide.

173

Answer Key

Water Sports
Find and circle the words in the puzzle.

knife	mask	spear	aqua-lung
skiing	diving	wet suit	ropes
paddle	swimming	oxygen	float
polo			weights

174

Grocery Store Color Hunt
The grocery store is a colorful place. It is perfect for a color hunt! Bring this page with you the next time you go to the grocery store. Look for foods that match each color shown below. Write what you find next to its color.

Answers will vary.

175

Texture Hunt
Peel the paper off of a dark crayon. Grab a few pieces of paper and head outside.

Lay the paper against tree trunks, sidewalks, and patio furniture. Look for anything else that has an interesting texture. Rub the crayon over the paper to copy the textures.

Cut out a square from each texture. Paste the squares in the grid below. Then, ask a friend to guess where each rubbing came from.

Answers will vary.

176

What's Different?
Can you spot the 10 differences in these two pictures?

177

Community Helpers
Find and circle the words in the puzzle.

firefighter	dentist	mechanic
doctor	teacher	baker
nurse	clerk	plumber
bus driver	judge	barber

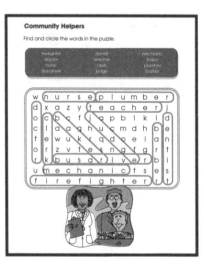

178

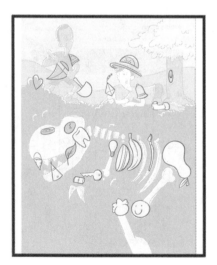

181

255

Answer Key

Machine Search

Find and circle the words in the puzzle.

car, plane, motorcycle, drill, typewriter, jet, crane, saw, lathe, tractor, motor, toaster, computer, punch

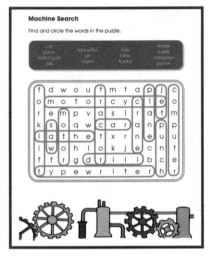

182

What's Different?

Can you spot the 12 differences in these two pictures?

183

Sports Search

Find and circle the words in the puzzle.

volleyball, tennis, cheerleading, swim, soccer, softball, cross country, gymnastics, dance

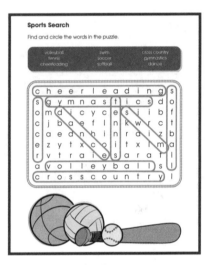

185

Fashion Frenzy

Find and circle the words in the puzzle.

sunglasses, scarf, sundress, mittens, shorts, coat, boots

187

Scavenger Hunt

An Arctic tern has been migrating through the pages of this book. Can you find all the pages it has flown through?

List the 14 pages on the lines below.

13 21 45 58 81 90 96

124 136 142 166 193 202 224

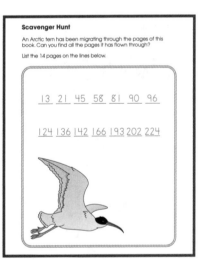

188

Hidden Message

Find the words from the word bank in the puzzle. Color them. Then, starting at the top and moving from left to write, find the letters that are left in the puzzle. Write the letters on the lines below. They will spell out a secret message. Do what the message tells you to do!

run, leaps, jump, fun, wiggle, hop, squat, bounce, dance

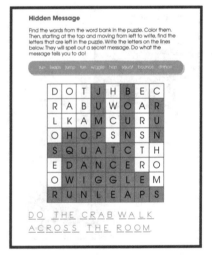

DO THE CRAB WALK
ACROSS THE ROOM.

239